ANTONY COPLEY

A MEMOIR

HISTORIAN AND HOMOSEXUAL: SEARCH FOR A POSTWAR IDENTITY

Edited Diaries and Journals

An environmentally friendly book printed and bound in England by
www.printondemand-worldwide.com

FastPrint Publishing
http://www.fast-print.net/bookshop

HISTORIAN AND HOMOSEXUAL:
SEARCH FOR A POSTWAR IDENTITY

A catalogue record for this book is available from the British Library

ISBN 978-178456-297-7

First published 2015 by
FASTPRINT PUBLISHING
Peterborough, England.

For Elizabeth Harper, who listened
and
Rashid Maxwell, who dared

The Author at 77

Antony Copley is Honorary Professor of Modern European and Indian History at the University of Kent. He qualified as a teacher in Modern European History at St Antony's College and is a self-taught Indian historian. At home he taught at UCNW, Bangor 1963-66 and the University of Kent 1967-2001. In universities abroad: the Jawaharlal Nehu University, Monsoon Semester 1973, Ibadan 1974-5; Nankai, Tianjin 1988; Visiting Professor at Venkateswara University, Tirupati, Central University, Hyderabad and the University of Bangalore 1995; Professeur Invité, University of Paris 8 St Denis 1998. His historical interests are decolonisation, sexual liberation and religion and the spiritual. Publications on Europe include *Sexual Moralities in France 1780-1980* (Routledge 1989) and *Music and the Spiritual: Composers and Politics in the 20th Century* (Ziggurat 2012). On India two monographs on Indian independence leaders, *The Political Career of C. Rajagopalachari 1937-54* (Macmillan 1978) and *Gandhi: Against the Tide* (Blackwell 1987 and OUP 1993), a study of Protestant Evangelicals in 19th century India *Religions in Conflict* (OUP 1997), two editions on the Indian Religious Reform Movements, *Gurus and their Disciples* (OUP 2000) and *Hinduism in Public and Private* (OUP 2003). His major work was *A Spiritual Bloomsbury* (Lexington 2006), a study of the way three English writers, Edward Carpenter, E M Forster and Christopher Isherwood engaged with Hindu spirituality. He still reviews frequently for *The Journal of the*

Royal Asiatic Society. He is Academic Adviser to the Gandhi Foundation UK.

Acknowledgements

I thank Pauline Barker, archivist at Kingshott School for sending me a copy of the original school curriculum, Liz Darby, archivist at Gresham's School, for information on my Father's time at the school. I thank Neil Cheshire for letting me see his *Festschrift* on May Davidson and information on the Warneford Hospital. Conversations with Richard Vinen clarified my thoughts on National Service. I thank Rachel Forrester-Jones for her invitation to give a grass roots lecture in Rutherford College on my National Service. I am very grateful to all those who read the manuscript and for their critical response: Rod Kedward, Hugh Maddox, Neil Cheshire, Hugh and Diane Cunningham, Elizabeth Harper, Michael Williams. I thank Pauline Tebbutt for steering me through the demands of publishing. Without the help of Trish Hatton the book would never have seen the light of day.

Contents

1
PREFACE

I have always rather mocked those who enclose round robin letters with their Christmas cards. How can one possibly be interested in all those children and relatives one does not know, or respond appropriately to all those activities? And yet now I have written a kind of large scale round robin letter in this memoir, and why should anyone be interested?

Superficially mine is a fairly typical life story of a son of the professional middle class with a predictable journey through preparatory and public school, my generation then doing National Service, and so onto University - Oxbridge in my case. All of this would form a rather unpleasant, overbearing kind of person. In fact there was little that was straightforward and at all stages there was to be conflict and distress.

Adolescence is overshadowed by a search for identity. It is a difficult choice whether to explore this search retrospectively and so highlight all those obvious turning points which determine this quest, or alternatively, see it as far more subject to chance. In retrospect two major identities were to emerge. I was to become an academic historian. This can be traced quite easily and I was tempted to entitle this memoir *The Making of a Modern Historian*. I had to decide whether to remain a mediaeval historian, the focus of my undergraduate work, or move onto the modern field, in fact the focus of my graduate studies and future academic career. The other identity was a sexual one and by the end of this memoir I have accepted myself as a homosexual. If much harder to trace, I could simply accept that this was always going to be a future identity and again point to decisive moments when this identity was predictable. It raises of course the issue of nature over nurture. All this would guarantee, as one of my friends has put it, we would always be aware of the big picture.

But what if all this is misleading? What if our future identity is far more unpredictable and indeed our lives are subject to the uncertainty principle, even fate? Our lives could take any number of directions. If studying History was invariably my strongest subject I can find no evidence I ever had a vocation to be a historian, and, indeed, I seem at several junctures to have sought some alternative academic interest. Maybe English anyway always ran it close and here were the beginnings of a powerful belief from late school days onwards, that I had a vocation to be a poet. At the same time religion became a grave preoccupation and if my attraction to the monastic life was never very strong, here was yet another possible solution to an identity crisis. And then at Oxford, faced by the trauma that lies at the heart of this memoir, I discovered a strong calling to be a psychotherapist.

It is now widely recognised that our sexuality lies on a wide spectrum from outright homosexuality to outright heterosexuality. Would it not be truer to say our sexual identity remains very fluid throughout adolescence? And I tend to reject a merely genetic inheritance and favour an account which explores parental relationships and the unpredictable circumstances of our upbringing. I rather like the way E M Forster decided in adolescence. Sitting in front of the sitting room window he decided that the next person that passed would indicate his future preference. It happened to be a man.

Are we in any way shaped by our ancestry? Does this at most tell us something about the personality of our parents? I pay lip service to the convention of these personal memoirs of tracing the family background. In my Father's case this certainly pointed to the career choice he might make, between the law and banking. Did my Mother's background in trade explain a certain snobbery in the family? Very clearly my parents were profoundly shaped by their own childhoods and their parents. My Father was driven inwards by family tragedy and became a person who was absolutely determined to make his own way in life. My Mother was always under the spell of family and much of her life was simply devoted to family, her Mother above all, and a wish to keep up with her far more practical and worldly elder sister, Auntie Betty.

And just how much did I take from my parents? I was far closer to my Mother in childhood and was clearly a mother's boy. Early on fears were being expressed that I was in danger of becoming a pansy. Yet as I grew older my relationships with my Mother became conflicted. I was often infuriated by her values. She set such a high standard on appearance, dress codes, the proprieties of social behaviour. In no way did she share my own interest in high culture and travel. However I can detect in myself a shared tendency to fault others, a certain cantankerousness. I was never emotionally close to my Father and ours was, in adolescence, in many ways a disturbing and strange relationship. Obviously I was led by his example to pursue a professional career, if not as he so strongly wished, the law, but academe. There was another rather odd indebtedness. Father's greatest compliment of others was to say they were normal. I seemingly absorbed this love of normality. My favoured description of my lovers was to describe them as ordinary blokes. Long into my relationship with the last of my companions, Brian, I recognised how curiously similar he and my Father were in the face. Had I finally married my Father?

And yet writing this memoir has filled me with remorse about my parents. I have read all our correspondence, many letters from my Mother, far fewer from my Father, and I realise now how little justice I did them in their lifetime. My Mother did wonders in terms of looking after my step-father, Vivian, born with a weak heart. He was a generous but feckless man and always a worry to her. She also bore the burden of looking after my sad sister, though this was always a love-hate relationship and a trial to them both. I now wonder if my Father did not want to discuss his troubled professional career and I missed an opportunity to be closer to him.

But my saddest memory of all is my sister Georgina. I say little in the memoir about her. She had such a zest for life but this did nothing to spare her endless knocks. I read again all her voluminous letters and realise now how perceptive an observer she often was. Her letters from South Africa are of particular interest, an initially rosy-eyed view but coming to see the obscenities of apartheid. She was a travelling salesperson for various beauty consultants and got to know both the Indian community in Durban well, and her black driver. I rather suspect she was going to be deported before an attempted suicide forced her return anyway. Later, following an appalling car crash, she became bi-polar and was on medication for the rest of her life. Of all people she is the one I most look forward to meeting on the other side.

Seeing my childhood cut short by going to my prep school at the age of 7, I then enter a period of pre-adolescence. Quite when this turns into adolescence proper I'm unsure. But this is the time of my two boarding schools, Kingshott and Gresham's. In many ways these are weird stories, with a mad headmistress in the first and a histrionic and unhinged headmaster in the second. Maybe the events of the school take precedence over any account of my emergence as a historian and the uncertainties of my sexuality. But I do describe the highly privileged education these schools offered, above all in the Sixth Form at Gresham's, Eric Kelly in History, Hoult Taylor in English. Between them I was to win an Open Scholarship to Oxford, key to the future.

Then came National Service. This chapter I wrote quite independently, partly in response to an invitation to give a so-called Grass Roots lecture at Rutherford College, University of Kent, a chapter in one's personal life, partly to clarify my own experience of National Service for

Richard Vinen, who interviewed me several times for his definitive study *National Service: Conscription in Britain 1945-1963*. If this was the most different experience of my life it does however closely connect. My experience of late imperialism, the Cyprus Emergency and Suez, did much to explain my later engagement with the history of decolonisation. And the oppressive attitude to homosexuality in the Navy also contributed to my commitment to the story of sexual liberation.

One memory stands out. A CPO had been arrested on HMS Forth for gross indecency. He had been deported back to England. Staggeringly, the Navy chose to send him, chained to the hold of a destroyer, all the way to Suez for court-martial. I witnessed this. He appeared almost insane. He was a broken man.

But National Service was also the time I pursued ideas fashioned in the Sixth form and there is a difficult chapter on this intellectual odyssey. I was caught up in a debate, never wholly understood at the time, between what I now see as an other-worldly vision of T S Eliot and an attempt by Stephen Spender to present a counter this-worldly philosophy. Spender saw Eliot's attempt to reach out to the transcendental as the destructive principle, a fatal betrayal of the merely human. Oddly it was to be this very theme I turned to in retirement for my book on music, *Music and the Spiritual: Composers and Politics in the 20th Century*. It was a time I took to writing poetry. I had the good fortune to be able to listen to a great deal of music in the home of John and Emily Craig, related to my step-mother. I was also working through much questioning of religion. And thanks to the visits of the Navy to Italy I was beginning to learn a great deal about European painting.

And so to Oxford in 1957 and the trauma that lies at the heart of this memoir. Worcester College was still very public school and only at the beginnings of the successful attempt by David Mitchell to convert it into a more mixed college and more academic. But I was fortunate in my History tutors, the newly appointed mediaevalist, James Campbell, one of Keith McFarlane's most brilliant pupils and Harry Pitt, the Modern History Fellow, lively and provocative, to become a great ally in my life. The memoir traces my very ambivalent attitude to the study of history. I was never a sentimentalist about Oxford and maybe for obvious reasons.

In my second summer term 1958, I was arrested on a charge of gross indecency. I was a victim of police entrapment. I suffered a severe breakdown and spent time in the Warneford hospital. I will not anticipate here my account of this ordeal. I have had to take difficult decisions about exploring the confused sexuality that led to this trauma. It may seem morbid and retrograde to dwell on this conviction in the pre-1967 days when homosexuals existed in a reign of terror. We have moved on so remarkably since. I have to admit to a certain nostalgia for those days and have never wholly been at ease in the commercialised world of gay sexuality opened up by the pink pound. I feel that if in any way reading this memoir is helpful to anyone who had to endure the same trauma, then it has been a worthwhile venture. I have also been intrigued to assess how the trauma and the treatment at the Warneford affected the trajectory of my life.

I was very fortunate in being awarded a Senior Scholarship at St Antony's College. This was a new graduate college, still finding its way, and a very beguiling time to be there. Here I made the decision to be a historian though still not without a considerable debate. And this seems the sensible point to complete a memoir on adolescence, though I look a little further ahead to the universities of Bangor and Kent. And this is the time when I ran out of access to my private journals, the main source of the memoir.

At a later stage I came deeply under the influence of Hindu philosophy. I was persuaded that the ego is an illusion and that it dissolves into *samsara*, like, as Ramakrishna put it, the salt doll into the sea. It was an idea put to brilliant use by Christopher Isherwood in his novel *A Single Man*. But clearly I could not write this memoir with such thoughts in mind. At the time I am writing about I fell under the influence of Freud and delighted in his dramatic account of a three way struggle between ego, superego and id. Far more of this outlook underpins the memoir.

But there is another source of impermanence. I am writing at a time of recurrent prostate cancer. The hormone therapy knocks out testosterone, so I am living with a form of chemical castration. In some ways this is pleasing as it puts paid to what Auden called 'the intolerable neural itch'. You acquire, thanks to the pharmaceutical industry, a Buddhist sense of desirelessness. But it may distance me from writing about my homosexuality, so central to my life.

It has been tempting in looking back at all the foibles which my adolescent journals reveal, to become my own fiercest critic, but I have resisted this. The story has to tell itself.

2
PARENTS

Is there any biography or autobiography that does not begin with family history? Is there some uncritical assumption that tracing one's family tree has to reveal something about the character of the subject in question? All too frequently it tells us little, but we persist. More can obviously be read into the story of the nuclear family, though invariably this is interpreted in negative terms. Yet even here surely much is merely speculative about all those repressions. But all this has to be addressed. We tend also to focus on the nuclear family in terms of childhood, but surely these tensions last on into adulthood and are here of equal significance. Our relationship with our parents never ceases. It is almost embarrassing the way children talk about their parents long into adulthood: indeed our preoccupation with parents is often stronger in old age, no doubt through our memories of the past growing ever stronger at the expense of the more recent. I must have thrashed out the difficulties of my relationships with my parents a quite excessive amount of time, either with the two psychotherapists I've encountered or with friends. Is one ever the wiser? Is this energy wasted? Yet the dynamic of childhood was real. In later life I kept up enough contact with both parents to ward off any sense of guilt at their neglect. Now I regret not knowing them better.

My Mother, Iris Miriam Pohlman, was born 7 December 1913. At that time the family name was spelt Pohlmann. The second 'n' was only dropped during the First World War through the popular xenophobia against Germans. The family followed the example of the Saxe-Coburgs. She was born at 64a Eynham Road, a home birth, now in White City, then Kensington, and registered in the sub-district of North Hammersmith. So did my Mother grow up in London? The Pohlman family do not know when my grandparents moved to Hertford. My maternal grandfather, George Cecil Pohlman, is recorded on the birth certificate as a Motor Manufacturer Salesman and, indeed, he did work for one of London's grander showrooms, but in time he set up his own garage and showroom in Hertford. At first he was a dealer in Armstrong-Siddeleys and Triumphs, later Rovers and Bentleys. All models my Father was to buy from him.

My Pohlman cousins have been assiduous in tracing the Pohlman family tree. Back in Austria and Germany they made pianofortes. There was a Gabriel Pohlmann in Vienna, possibly 1642-93, then a Johann Christoff and he moved the family business to Steinhorst in Hanover. Was it the same who moved the family business to Soho in 1765 and then onto Harrogate in the 1790s? There they joined the society of quite wealthy tradesmen and craftsmen. This family firm continued on into the 20th century, refused to convert the factory into making war materials at the outset of the Second World War, switched instead to sheet music and radios. As late as the 1980s the family estate was being sold off.

Meanwhile a branch of the family firm had been set up in Davis Street, Dublin and there I pick up the story of Grandpa Pohlman. It seems he rejected taking over the Dublin branch and left Dublin for Cork to become involved in the new motor trade. He had been educated at Bedford School, had been a brilliant sportsman, later an accomplished golfer. It was in Dublin that he met, seduced and married Ethel Sophie Harrison, he but 24, she 22. There seems little doubt that she was already pregnant. My Uncle Vernon was born in 1909. Cecil was good looking and highly personable but seen as a patriarch, and one of my cousins sees him as loathsome.

The Harrison family is being extensively researched, a doctoral thesis on them shortly to be submitted. Their most distinguished ancestor was John Harrison, inventor of the longitudinal clock. To quote one commentary, 'a maverick and a genius', who managed to extract most of the reward of £20,000 from the Board of Longitude, worth several million today. He also invented late in life a mechanical clock, scorned at the time but recently proven to be incredibly accurate. But here I need go no further back than Charles Harrison, who set up a family firm of ecclesiastical stone masons in 178 Great Brunswick Street - the High Altar and pulpit in Newry Cathedral, and carvings in the Royal College of Science amongst his artefacts. He was a Member of the Architectural Association of Ireland, the Royal Dublin Society, the Masonic order, the Corinthian Club, the Company of St Patrick. He died at the age of 55 and was succeeded as head of the family firm by my great-great-maternal grandfather, Charles Lloyd Harrison. Much has been made of his marrying into a distinguished Huguenot family by his marriage to Jessie Mercer. In 1674 the Irish Parliament had granted Huguenots the right of settlement. Obviously this strengthened the Protestant loyalties of the family and helps to explain why my grandparents left for England, the Easter Rising the writing on the wall. The Protestant Dublin elite were one casualty of Irish independence. The firm is listed as specialists in all architectural church work, polished granite shop fronts. The business was not however to die out. The Harrisons converted to Catholicism and I was to meet the family on a walking holiday in Wicklow in the 1980s where they now live.

Granny Pohlman was one of a large family, five children listed in the 1901 census, to Charles and Jessie. She was brought up in 34 Park Avenue, Dublin, though the family moved. I was astonished to learn that her Mother lived to the ripe old age of 87, dying 24 November 1951. I also learnt of her younger brother Eddie, poet and lover of poetry, who went on to captain boats for the Santa Catalonia Island Company, be a Lieutenant-Commander in the American Coast Guard and fight in naval transport in the Pacific in the Second World War. He lived as long as 16th October 1992. Her brother Jack married a musical star, Ouida McDermott, but she left him, and he married his Catholic secretary, Connie Ryson and this explains the conversion of the Harrisons to Catholicism. All this suggests a certain risqué quality to Granny's family. She was strikingly beautiful and no doubt Grandpa was himself readily seduced. She was only ever a housewife and possibly here was Mother's role model. Certainly my

Mother had no stronger loyalty than to family. But did she otherwise inherit anything from this background?

My Father was born 20 January 1908. Grandfather Harry Copley, a distinguished Solicitor in St Ives and Huntingdon, was 40 at the time. Grandpa was born 1867, son of Robert Copley, a bank clerk. The Copleys seem to have alternated between banking and the law. I grew up believing we were related to the American painter, John Singleton Copley and that were I to announce in Copley Square, Boston that I was a Copley, the traffic would grind to a halt. But I cannot make the connection. The famous Boston portrait painter was persuaded to come to England in 1774 by Benjamin West and to convert to being a history painter, and, indeed, in Hanover Square was to paint such famous paintings as the Death of the Earl of Chatham, the Arrest of the Five Members of the Commons by Charles 1st, the Offer of the Crown to Lady Jane Grey. But he fell out of favour with his Equestrian Portrait of the Prince Regent. His son, another J S Copley, went on to enjoy a brilliant legal career and become Lord Chancellor, so it is just possible here was the origin of the Copleys as lawyers.

The family were evidently immensely proud of their marriage into the distinguished Hanchett family. Robert Copley married Harriet Hanchett. We appropriated the Hanchett family crest, three erect right hands, and almost all of us added the Hanchett name. I did so in my adult baptism in Gresham's School chapel. Out of family snobbery? Almost certainly of Norman background, the Hanchetts contributed to the Norman yoke. In time they owned considerable estates on the Cambridgeshire and Hertfordshire border as well as in Yorkshire.

But there were even more exceptional forms of ownership on my paternal grandmother's side. Sophie Marion Hart was born in 1867, one of three children of Charles Hart, a stationer in Ramsgate. Although I've been unable to trace the link, she was almost certainly the granddaughter of John August Tulk. He had married Susanna Hart, siring 12 children, with five sons and two daughters surviving. He was a businessman with a conscience. He was interested in social reform, prisons and asylums, opposed capital punishment. He was a County Magistrate in Middlesex, 1836-47, MP for Sudbury 1820-26 and Poole in 1837. More intriguingly, he had an interest in literature and spirituality. He was a disciple of Coleridge and patron of William Blake. He took an interest in phrenology. He was attracted to Swedenborg and if he never actually joined the church, developed a rational mysticism in opposition to materialism. Here was a spiritual legacy of huge interest to my grandparents.

Family myth has it that once we had owned Leicester Square but lost it to gambling. It is true that John August Tulk had inherited an estate in Leicester Square but was no great business man and had lost his share in 1807. The property had been divided seven ways between his children. But his son, John Augustus Tulk, had retrieved half of the estate, and Granny continued to receive moneys from the estate till 1947. Here were funds that allowed her to go on foreign travel and there is in the records a P&O trip to Gibraltar. She was a lady of high culture and an accomplished painter, and she needed to escape the cultural limitations of her marriage. I was told one member of her family was a Professor of Languages in the University of Buenos Aires.

My Father's family experienced crippling bereavements. In many ways my Father was the most seriously affected by these. He was the third son, Uncle Bob and Uncle Fred older. Three years younger was George Douglas Copley. There was a disaster. Young George was taken on a walk by a maid to pick flowers for his younger brother, Geoffrey, they crossed a meadow in which there was a well with a defective cover, and George fell in. The maid panicked and fled. George drowned. (What happened to Geoffrey?) Later there was a stillborn daughter. These accumulated tragedies turned my grandparents to spiritualism, very much in vogue at the time. In their garden in St Ives there was a summer house with mysterious rooms lit by coloured bulbs, of great fascination to my sister and I, and here séances were held. My future Auntie Ann was to display great talents as a medium. A message came through that she was to marry Uncle Bob.

I came across an account of a visit to my grandparents in possibly December 1957. Grandpa talked of communications from the other side, though now it was Indians whereas once it had been Chinese mandarins. They told him some of his children were bastards. He could not answer them back but wished to go over to the other side to tell them they were wrong. He heard the messages, 'clear as a pikestaff'. (All the more remarkable as he was stone deaf.)

George was Father's favourite brother and he took his loss badly. He was to name two of his children after him, my sister Georgina and my half-brother, George. Such was the emotional burden on my grandparents that they decided to make their lives easier by dispatching my Father as a boarder to a school. Was this at the age of 4? Maybe a little older. This must have been a crippling emotional blow. He turned for support to Aunt Savory, my grandfather's sister, and she was his alternative mother figure. I've no doubt all of my Father's inability to handle his emotions, their repression, flowed from this family exile. His instinctive reaction to emotional demands was to turn away. Even so, he was a devoted son and always found time to visit his parents.

My mental image of both sets of grandparents tends to be of them in their later years and all lived into their eighties and nineties. It is always said we love our grandparents best of all, maybe because they were not authority figures but just loving relatives. In fact my only recollection as a child of corporal punishment was being beaten by Granny Copley with a hairbrush. Granny Pohlman became very plump but always regal and well dressed. I saw her as a matriarch and she certainly commanded the respect and, indeed, in the case of Betty, my Mother and Uncle Edgar, their devotion. I find it hard to see Grandpa Pohlman as the patriarch. I recall him as a rather quiet withdrawn older man, with a heavily-lined face and reeking of tobacco. Surely no one saw him as other than an old-fashioned gentleman? My sister, however, recalled their family rows when younger, of Granny hiding in tears under the bed and refusing to come out till Grandfather abandoned his affair with his secretary. It seems both my grandfathers were flirts. Grandpa Copley was said to flirt with the family's long time domestic servant and cook, Louie, much to the chagrin of Granny. But the question remains, to what extent did my grandparents shape the lives of my parents?

I have very little idea of my Mother's life before her marriage to my Father. She was the third child, after Vernon and Betty, and much of her life was an attempt to live up to the standards of her elder sister. Betty was always in touch with the latest styles. But she was also, unlike my Mother, very competent in business - she ran a successful restaurant in Basingstoke - and in the ways of the world. Both sisters were very protective of their younger brother, Edgar, one of my most sympathetic and favourite relatives. Theirs was a life-time devotion to their Mother. Mother went to a convent school though her level of education was not high. I know of few people who took so little interest in high culture. She loved reading fashion magazines and Country Life. Was she good at games? I remember her once saying she was good at lacrosse. I think she was a tolerable tennis player. Such education as she had prepared her for no employment and the only job I'm aware she ever had, and that was but brief, was modelling hats. Did she only ever entertain the idea of marriage? And she was to display strong household skills, not so much as a cook but in decorating a home. Somewhere she acquired a knowledge and taste for antiques (though when I came to clear her last flat, sadly it emerged that much of her furniture were copies). She was good at flower displays. All her homes were, if conventional, beautifully laid out. Much of her ferocious energy was put into keeping them clean and tidy.

She was strikingly beautiful. I have in mind two photographs. One is of my Mother carrying baby Georgina. Hers is a firm, strongly featured face, shortish curled black hair, Mother smiling into the distance, a thin top lip, fuller lower, perfect teeth, a well-shaped chin and a smaller nose than was usually the case with the Pohlmans. Another photo I discovered, in a black metal box I inherited from my step-father, is of Mother naked to the waist, with perfectly shaped breasts and short cut hair. I assume this was taken when Mother, after the divorce, disappeared from my life. My memory is rather of her with longer hair, not quite shoulder length, somewhat softer in the face, and bearing a striking resemblance to Margaret Lockwood. When I see old films of the actress, such as Hitchcock's *The Lady Vanishes,* there is my Mother. Maybe my generation watch old movies just because they remind us of our parents. My own photographs are all postwar, but one - Mother in angora sweater - for obvious Freudian reason, stands out. Mother, in fact, rather dreaded having her photo taken, no doubt worried that she was not looking at her best. Mother lived by appearances. Looks were paramount. My sister always saw her as vain and I do recall, once driving her, her checking herself constantly in the vanity mirror. If conventionally so, she was always stylishly dressed. I can recall frequent visits to London to purchase the latest fashion in shoes, high-heeled, though clunky looking.

Given my Mother's preoccupations with appearance it is not surprising she was also a social snob. Although her family were wealthy enough to see themselves as middle class, theirs was a background of trade, so maybe they had some social leeway to make up. Mother certainly believed in public schools and the old school tie. May be this explains why she set her cap at a professional lawyer who looked as if he might become rich.

My Mother always looked after herself. She always ate sensibly and watched her weight. She does not seem to have inherited Granny's tendency to put on weight, the bane of my poor sister's life. She lived to 89. Compare this with her siblings. Auntie Betty went on absurd diets and was too weak to resist surgery at the age of 70. Uncle Edgar smoked himself to an early death from cancer. But this is anticipating.

I have no photograph of my Father prior to his marriage, none indeed till the 1940s. This emotionally starved boy only takes on some appearance from his going to Gresham's. His parents had obviously got word of this progressive school in Norfolk and sent Father there. Uncle Bob had gone to Haileybury. In the school records Father was at Old School House, then the junior house, and so to Kenwyn, 1919-24. For Father, always favouring maths and science, I'm intrigued to discover in 1919 he was awarded the second form prize in English and History. In 1923, though, he won a prize for maths. Otherwise the record is on games, his playing rugby, cricket and hockey for

Kenwyn, and cricket for the school in 1924, though I don't quite see how that could have been. Quite young, he was made a sub-prefect. I wonder what he said when he spoke in a debate on advertising, to be the subject much later of an idiotic row between us. I am more interested to know quite how in the long term he incorporated into his own moral code the Gresham's code of honour, every boy agreeing to avoid swearing, smoking, and any indecent behaviour, with that fatal caveat of reporting any such misdemeanours to his housemaster. He clearly retained the greatest respect for his headmaster, Mr Eccles. He was to put me down for the school at birth. But he left at the tender age of 16 to train as a lawyer.

Again I can only guess at how he grew up with his family. He was always jealous of his elder brother, Bob, quite unfairly treated as their favourite by his parents. But he tagged along with Bob, shared a dare-devil love of motor-bikes, played rugby together. Father was in fact a considerable player, an outside half, and a large part of adolescence was spent with his male friends, playing home and abroad for Parkhouse. One of his trademarks was sending home greetings from abroad on beer labels. One of the consequences of his being distanced from his Father was his determination to go it alone and be a self-made lawyer. Bob was to work in the family firm. Grandfather lent my Father £100 to set up his first office in Burnt Oak but the money was to be repaid in six months. Grandfather, however, always recognised that Father was the better lawyer and was to consult him in later life on how to draw up his will.

But Father's legal career began with a major set-back. He had got to know the parents of Freddie Hails and was persuaded that their son should be his legal partner. But Freddie Hails then embezzled their clients' moneys, and Father had to struggle to pay this back. Even so, all his working life he retained the title of Hanchett Copley and Hails. They had tossed a coin as to which would join the army on the outbreak of war and Freddie won (or lost). Father in fact took up a far tougher role, joining the fire service, and during the blitz was to break his back. He was cursed all his life with lumbago. But meanwhile he had met my Mother.

He was a handsome man. As a child I likened him to Alan Ladd. Later he morphed into Anthony Eden and then Harold Macmillan. This run of prime ministers broke down with Douglas-Home. I have no recollection of him without a moustache (though he never sported a beard). He had gingerish hair, a rounded rather than aquiline face and an athlete's frame. He played a lot of tennis and was a good golfer. However he had to abandon the latter as fellow Masons pestered him on the course for free legal advice. My favourite photograph of him is with his fishing rod, our dachshund Lisa at his feet, smoking a pipe, a smiling and happy man. I must have taken this photo. Fishing was his great hobby and nothing gave him greater pleasure than getting away from it all, preferably, I think, on his own. I did join him once or twice but proved quite abject as a fly-fisherman. Later photographs show him far more morose. For all the bonhomie he showed, propping up a bar, in company, there was a conflicted and anxious man beneath. My step-mother had to work hard to prevent a complete breakdown in the 1970s. The job had got on top of him. He had planned retirement but the hike in oil prices and serious inflation had eroded his pension provision and almost certainly staying on an extra three years contributed to his heart attack.

I have some idea how my parents met. Father had courted Vera, to be the wife of my Mother's elder brother, Vernon. This was how he met, as my step-mother puts it, the fast set of the Pohlman sisters. Father was first attracted to Betty, the more glamorous and far more confident of the two sisters. So why Iris? Well, my Mother became pregnant. What to do? Cecil and Ethel decided that Father was the most promising of Mother's paramours and that was that. On the 12 January 1935 they were married. Was it a white wedding? On 23 June Georgina was born. So it is just possible she was but my half-sister, but I think not. It was a prolonged and difficult birth and I suspect this explains the future conflicted relationship between mother and daughter.

Was it always a doomed marriage? Their shared interests were minimal. Mother took no interest in Father's legal affairs and refused to entertain his clients. She was only ready to entertain her family. I doubt if she ever went to a rugby match and never accompanied him on his fishing weekends. But then I doubt if he ever took much interest in her domestic skills. Nor can I ever visualise them sharing a bedroom. In my mind's eye Mother is always alone in her bedroom in The Trees, the family home of my childhood. But then the spare room where I recall my Father sleeping was billeted out to soldiers during the war. Anyway, I was conceived sometime in November 1936, born 1 July 1937. It was a very easy birth.

Maternal Grandfather

Maternal Grandmother with Antony & sister, Georgina (left) - 1945

Paternal grandparents

Mother - 1946

Father

Mother at 18

Father – 1949

Father – 1950

Mother

Father - 1951

Mother

Mother - 1950

Father - 1948

House 'Barnes House' (St Ives)

House 'The Trees' (Elstree)

3
CHILDHOOD

The new science of epigenetics claims that during the first seven years of life, through the way as children we observe parents, siblings, the community, traits are laid down which determine our future outlook on life. Here is the source of high or low self-esteem. Can memory recall that early conditioning? For many children of the professional middle class it is at 7 years old, with their being dispatched to boarding school, that childhood ends. There is a fatal rupture with their family. Can children somehow undo that early conditioning? Quite when childhood ends is questionable. Is it with the first act of masturbation, a loss of innocence? And of course childhood is above all how we get on with our parents. I think in my case going to boarding school was indeed a hiatus but to discuss my relationship with my parents, I will still extend the experience of childhood on into my early teens.

Autobiographies are suffused with Proustian evocations of place. But a suburban childhood between the banality of Borehamwood and the village of Elstree provides no such inspiration. At the time of my birth we lived in Deacon's Hill Road but no doubt, needing now an extra room, moved to Barham Avenue. At the time this was still in the green belt, woods and fields to one side, the railway behind, and, at the end of the avenue, backing onto fields.

By this route one came to the railway bridge, one my sister, my cousin, Biddy - she stayed with us during the war - and I all crossed to reach our infant convent school. We used to love running in and out of the steam. Today the avenue is swallowed up in housing and greater Borehamwood. Even as a child I had some fear that this would be the case. I used to enjoy the walk to Elstree, passing a pigsty and stroking their spiky backs, and then by a bridle path to the village and St Lawrence, its church.

Were we the first occupants of The Trees, a detached 30s house set in a substantial garden? Here is a house whose layout I can vividly recall. My L-shaped room was in the front with a large window facing the road and a small side window that let me see down into the lounge. Adjacent was the upstairs loo and bathroom. Opposite was the spare room, which I always associated with my Father, then my sister's room, and then my Mother's large bedroom. The whole house was L-shaped. From the front door one entered into a hall with its grandfather clock, to the left at the back the kitchen and pantry, a utility room to the front, converted at times into a room for maids or housekeeper, then the dining room with a hatch to the kitchen, and finally the lounge. We never called it the sitting room. Then there was a large garden, given over to lawns and a rockery the length of the front, and to the back and side, extensive vegetable gardens and fruit orchards. I used to knock down nuts from the almond tree in the rockery. Helping myself to gooseberries - very prickly - strawberries, raspberries, peaches, plums was one of the furtive joys of childhood. Georgina and I were given a small patch to ourselves. We would grow seed in the garage. My limits as a gardener seemed to be the planting of wall-flowers. My Father was a dedicated and gifted gardener, though had help from full-time gardeners. The first was a Welshman, Mr Yorith, the second Mr Greenaway. They were to feature in my life.

Both my parents liked pets, dogs more than cats, but we had both. First of the dogs I recall were two middling-sized mongrels, Peter and Simon. Peter lived to a ripe old age. Quite why, I am unsure, but then we moved onto dachshunds. First was Lisa. I had a sadistic streak in me and relentlessly teased her and she spent a lot of time hiding under the furniture. Father was Lisa's favourite, but then he took her for walks and on his fishing weekends. In time she was joined by Polly, my late Grandmother Copley's dog, a mixture of who knows what, buck-teethed and mainly Pekinese. She also came into her fair share of teasing. Lisa in time was replaced by another dachshund, Maxi, an exceptionally aggressive dog: once inside Father's car he went berserk if any one approached. Georgina and I had our own pets, certainly rabbits, and also a tortoise.

In fact my earliest memories are far more associated with the houses of my grandparents than The Trees. War forced our migration. My maternal grandparents lived in Little Combles in Hertford, an ill-lit possibly Victorian house, set back from the road where my grandfather's garage and showroom were. No doubt the cedar tree in the front blocked out the light. In my memory it's a house full of faded brown leather furniture. There was one traumatic moment when my bedroom light bulb fell out, fire licked up the flex to the ceiling and Granny rushed in to put out the flames. And, oddly, though this must be much later, I can recall Granny reporting the death of two pansies, her word, likewise through an electrical fault, in their electric blanket. But Hertford was bombed and we migrated further out of the reach of the war to my paternal grandparents house in St Ives. All of Little Combles has since disappeared, pulled down to make way for new road systems in the town.

Barnes House was a substantial Victorian building opposite the beautiful Anglican Church in St Ives. It borders on the River Ouse. It was a rambling house, the major rooms being the dining room which doubled up as the sitting room, and behind a strange room, full of bric-a-brac. I recall best a glass cage full of stuffed birds. It was here Granny beat me with a hair brush. Georgina and I had a constant struggle coping with the deafness of both grandparents. Upstairs we shared a room and here we suffered both measles and chickenpox. The garden was a great delight. There was of course that beguiling summer house. There were delicious figs, not a fruit in my Father's garden. The extraordinary thing is that we were allowed to roam at will on our own along the riverside, a freedom unimaginable today. Still, I cannot recall our making any friends. Barnes House still exists though I think it has lost its garden.

It was at Barnes House that I became literate. I owe this to our governess, Miss Toon. I think she was probably the classic governess, a spinster, a dear old lady and I fear we both sorely tried her with our misbehaviour. She was to accompany us back to The Trees. I have a guilty memory of Georgina and I going on a walk up Deacon's Hill Road and then abandoning poor Toonie, so that she feared she had lost us. She lived to an advanced age and Father was able to tell her of my success in gaining a scholarship to Oxford.

Miss Toon's good work was to be continued by the nuns of Our Lady of Sion. Was this my convent-educated Mother's choice of school? My Father kept all my school records. It appears I was educated here from October 1942 to July 1944, when the reports cease. The first report read: Conduct, very good. Studies, good. Very promising. Language: Poetry, a good beginning. (Did we write poetry?) Drawing, a very good beginning. (Did they ever report on my talent for drawing bunny rabbits and crows?) Handiwork, a fair beginning. By December 1943, in a different layout, Progress in Studies: much improved. Reading, a great progress. Writing: good. Arithmetic: very good. Little change by March 1944. By July 1944, Arithmetic: could do better. (Ah, first signs of a later weakness.) But all this indicates we did not spend as long as I supposed with our grandparents but came back to the Trees in 1942.

We could not escape the war entirely. I hated having to wear a gas mask. We took shelter under the stairs. I recall looking at doodle bugs. An incendiary bomb had fallen in a neighbouring wood, forming a pond where we used to play. But otherwise I have little recollection of the war. In many ways this was a care-free childhood.

There were family holidays. On the beautiful beach at Abersoch in North Wales there was a trauma. Someone on the beach persuaded my Father he could teach me how to swim. This took the form of dragging me down the beach and letting me go into the sea. I sank to the bottom and might have drowned. I did not learn to swim till I was 13. But the North Wales holidays were a delight. We learnt to ride on the beach but horses and I never really got on. I remember wonderful milk puddings. Did all this foreshadow my accepting my first academic post at UCNW, Bangor in 1963? On our holiday in Bournemouth I recall our scavenging the beach for coins and making quite a killing. And in Plymouth, quite when I do not remember, Georgina and I absconded from our lodgings to go on the bumper cars, much to the anger of Mother on our very late return. My favourite outings from home were going on picnics, often as part of our going to point-to-points.

Georgina and I were close during childhood. As babies when we were wheeled about in our joint pram, people stopping to admire our beauty, and, as Pope Gregory would have said, not Angles but Angels. Maybe at some level she never forgave me for displacing her as the only child, though she was always to remain Father's favourite. Another trauma was her locking me in my toy chest, no doubt the source of all future feelings of claustrophobia. But despite customary sibling rivalry we were good companions and fellow conspirators. She would put me up to mischief. I used to waddle up the avenue behind a bow-legged neighbour, cruelly imitating her disability. Georgina acted as watchdog while I stole one by one a whole series of illustrated histories of British history from Woolworths. My future as a historian was based on theft. Georgina was a film addict and I used to steal into her bedroom to look at terrifying images of Boris Karloff as Frankenstein and Christopher Lee as Dracula. But my sister displayed early signs of hysteria, had the most appalling temper, often expressed in rows with my Mother, and this was frightening and somewhat overshadowed our whole relationship.

We made friends with other children in the avenue, in particular with the Watts family. No doubt we got up to all kinds of mischief and invariably returned home muddy and the worse for wear. I can recall one occasion when we met a new playmate, a hermaphrodite - and I think we used the word - and we all stood around bemused by the sight of a boy with a vagina. But Mother's snobbism intervened. Mrs Watts ran a hardware shop in Borehamwood and so the family were not good enough for us. They were a bad influence. So I transferred my friendship to Richard, whose Mother shared Mother's interests in fashion, so he was acceptable. What would Mother have thought if she had known Richard and I used to store our urine in glass jars in the garden shed? Indeed, what was that all about?

So what kind of conditioning took place and was my relationships to my parents Oedipal? I had little or no sense of any emotional closeness, let alone physical intimacy, between my parents. Indisputably I was passionately in love with my Mother till going to boarding school. As a very young child, I was prone to nightmares, could not sleep without a night light, and craved a good night kiss from my Mother. Gifts entered early on into our relationship and I'd spend time and money on choosing Christmas and birthday presents from catalogues for toilet and beauty items. Mother had a good sense of humour and Georgina and I would be reduced to hysterics at her imagined slitting of her throat. She could be tough - she was very aggressive when washing my hair. And no doubt my Mother in her emotionally starved marriage did become too emotionally close to me. I once overheard someone warning my parents that I was in danger of becoming a mother's boy. Did all parents at the time secretly fear their sons would turn out to be 'pansies'? There was a mildly traumatic moment when in my Mother's bedroom Auntie Betty walked around with the flap of her jodhpurs open. Mother demurred but Betty said, 'he has to know some time, so why worry?' Was this rather alarming sighting of the female genitalia the roots of a later castration complex? Yet I have no recall of any incestuous feelings for my Mother.

If anything there was to be a reverse Oedipal complex, though I never hated my Mother. I was never close to my Father. I was just a little afraid of him. I can recall feeling very embarrassed at his smirking at my ineptitude at boning kippers. Was this the cause of my later technophobia? Father was really just someone who came and went to the office every day. He was always generous to his children and we lacked for nothing. But I recall no physical intimacy with my Father. How differently might my life have developed had he ever hugged me?

Somewhere there developed the condition of scoptophilia, voyeurism, the possible underlying source of all curiosity. I have a vivid recollection of seeing handsome Uncle Jack, Betty's husband, lolling in the bath with the most beautiful genitalia on display. It became an obsession to see men's genitalia, and not the little willies of my peers but those of adults, my Father included. So a very wayward behaviour began, my taking the opportunity to see them in public toilets, those tents at point-to-points, at Twickenham. Absolutely no-one was aware of this. I was very fortunate not to incur any risk, though once a paedophile did follow me from Borehamwood but fortunately gave up the chase before I reached home. I would have had no idea what he wanted.

Into this not unhappy family life came a moment of violent rupture when I was sent to boarding school in 1944. I'm seeing this at least partially as the end of childhood.

Antony & Georgina with Mother & Father - 1946

Antony & Mother - 1945

Antony & Father - 1952

Georgina - 1945

Georgina - 1950

Georgina - 1944

Georgina & Antony - 1944

Georgina – age 17

Antony & Georgina - 1946

Georgina & Antony - 1949

Antony & Georgina

Antony

Antony

Antony – 1944

Antony – 1944

Antony – 1949

Antony - 1952

4
KINGSHOTT SCHOOL 1944-50

By chance, taking a short cut to Radlett when the M1 was closed, I came across my old preparatory school, all of 60 years later. It was just recognisable. The school buildings now march up to the main road. When I arrived in 1944 (I'd assumed all my life it was 1945) it was well set back in a kind of park. The school today has 385 pupils, boys and girls: in my days on joining but a 100. It is currently divided into houses, Scott, Drake, Nelson, Pitt. I vividly recall Peter Scott coming to tell us about his bird reserves and I think this was my first awareness of flamingos, always to be my favourite bird. In the list of schools that its pupils now go on to, Gresham's does not feature. Was I the only Kingshott boy to go to Greshams? Apart from their name, there is little or nothing in common between today's Kingshott - flourishing, very much larger, highly regarded - and the school I attended in the 1940s.

The school was founded in 1931. It took its name from the story that King Henry VIII had hunted and shot here. The school building, Oakfield House, a Victorian building, though with the look of a Georgian, had been built in

1859. George Brabazon Stafford was its first headmaster, though truly his wife Christabel was equally its headmistress. She was all but to take over the running of the school in my time. Did they see in the school an emotional outlet for their childlessness? I wish I knew more about this tall, rather military looking man. He seems to have all but disappeared from the school's archives. Yet his values are written all over the school's original curriculum. Odd in a way that the school's decorative features should at its outset be highlighted: 'it is the headmaster's aim that every boy should appreciate the natural beauties of unstained wood and learn to appreciate them.' Well, there he succeeded, for I have always valued any natural wood in my various houses. A maximum amount of time was to be spent out of doors. And that was to be at some cost, for we had to endure the bitter winter of 1947. An emphasis was put on private activity. Boys, for example, could have a small garden of their own. (Is that why Father gave me one at home?)

So to the school's moral code. 'One of the most sensitive periods of development, if not the most sensitive, is passed through by a boy at his preparatory school. It is of the utmost importance that the different sides of his nature, physical, aesthetic, mental, and moral which receive their main bias here should have their fair share of stimulus and grow together. A general quickening of the faculties is aimed at so that the boys may discover their fullest line of happiness and of future service.' Creativity was given preference. The beliefs of C R Nevinson were drawn on, an artist admittedly no longer at his First World War best: 'in the use of hands lies human salvation'. The curriculum continues: 'these words are an inspiration, the truth of which can be simply seen - not only in the workshop, in artistic and musical activities, but in all hand-work done throughout the school.' 'The natural release of creative energy and balance of emotion are of obvious value in leisure time.' I was never to be good with my hands, but did make numerous toast racks as family presents and once a Penguin on wheels.

But formal work was important: 'disciplined routine work also has its place. This becomes sensible and vivid, of keen objective but not limited to one purpose. Such a workable harmony between what must be done for duty's sake and what must be done for the sheer joy of doing it, is of sound positive value and if found early, will be of lasting value.' I was of course quite unaware of these values at the time and I wonder now if my Father was won over by these objectives or just chose the school because he took to the personality of GBS. He was always to be very loyal to him. But did these values work their way through in my experience of the school? There is a quotation from Montaigne: 'the great and glorious masterpiece of man is to know how to live to purpose: all other things, to reign, to lay up treasure, to build, are at most but little appendices and props.'

Alex Renton has recently (the Observer 5 May 2014) published a highly damaging account of his time at Ashdown preparatory school in the 1970s. There was the abject misery of his first term, together with the threat from the 10 year old dormitory captain that he would whip him if he wept aloud. There was an absolute taboo on telling anyone outside the school how wretched it be. The headmaster threatened mass beatings, all letters home were censored. His is a history of psychological abuse, of 'attachment fracture', 'removing early emotional ties and building *esprit de corps*'. Here was a school, long after the passing of Empire, indoctrinating Victorian values, 'suppression of emotion, devotion to the team, distrust of women, and minimal empathy for the weak and ordinary'. Children were being taken too young from their family and home and denied 'the chance to love'. Renton saw in his five years at the school a 'deliberate crushing of our individuality, the suppression of emotional freedom'. Was Kingshott, some thirty years earlier, any better?

Indisputably this was an experience that cut me off from home life. Ever afterwards school and home were separate worlds. I have little recollection of being prepared for boarding school. So it was a trauma. I wept for nights on end and routinely wet my bed. I received no comfort whatever. Later, when I saw younger boys similarly wretched, I would try to comfort them. Relationships with my Mother were now on a new footing. I still craved her love but it was now exhibited through gifts. Her letters came together with sweets for my tuck box; Mother made the most delicious home-made fudge. There were also cuttings from the Daily Express of Rupert Bear - teddy bears were my greatest comfort at the time - and from the Mail of Rip Kirby. I returned the favour with gifts from beauty catalogues. I had never been emotionally close to my Father but by the time I left Kingshott I was addressing him as 'sir'. It was, however, only much later in my second spell of psychotherapy for cancer that I realised how drastic this loss of home had been to me.

Rather oddly, considering how little interest she took in high culture, Mother tried to improve my reading. She sent me novels by Walter Scott and Dickens. I have never really been able ever afterwards to read Scott but this early exposure to Dickens proved redeemable. I far preferred reading my Biggles books and those on Doctor Doolittle, let alone the comics *The Eagle* and its story of Dan Dare.

In time I must have been broken in. But there are painful memories. On the sports field I struggled to find any form at soccer. I was positioned all over the place. Once, on a freezing winter's day, I let in 8 goals in a school match. I was quite good as centre forward but in time found my natural position as centre half. I have no recall of early promise as a cricketer. GBS was keen on boxing but I hated it. I just recall being hit, in pain, nose bleeds and rather frightened. Another activity that filled me with dread was fire practice. One had to launch oneself from the top floor down a shoot but I was too nervous to let go of the rope and my hands got badly blistered.

Other memories are happier. I recall little of early teaching but do recall being congratulated in school assembly on my powers of observation of nature. I'd scored 100% in some natural history paper. There was Peter Scott's visit and a talk on his Wild Fowl Trust. There were plays. We did Chesterton's Little St Francis plays and I vaguely recall acting a dying Friar. Was I St Francis? I have little recall of how well I got on with the other boys but I do remember a Bigley, son of a Bedford Vicar, and our being very silly together, giggling during church services. Every Sunday we had to learn the Collect before being allowed access to our tuck box and then in Indian file we'd walk to St Ippolyts Church. I was also a treble soloist. Maybe I was just a rather silly at the time. But it was all to get a good deal more serious.

There was a far darker history to the school. This lay in the growing madness of Mrs Stafford and her increasingly totalitarian control of the school. No other word will do. In the first two years, from 8 to say 10 I was on the outside of her ruling circle, her Praetorian guard, but then I was included and became her No 1 enforcer. One memory stands out whilst an outsider. My parents always took me out at half-term and I looked forward to our having lunch in a rather good old coaching house hotel in nearby Stevenage. But on one of these occasions I had been caught red-handed by Mrs Stafford in stealing extra dates at breakfast. She accused me of doing so and though I lied, all the while trying to swallow the dates, I was exposed and immediately sent to the headmaster for punishment. I was threatened for the only time in my life with the cane. GBS was keen on corporal punishment and I'd often seen the red wheals on boy's bottoms. At this point my parents arrived. My Father used all his legal skills on my behalf. He pointed out if I were beaten before we went out for lunch I'd be miserable and spoil the day. If the beating was postponed till my return I would be anxious and this would equally throw a pall over the day. The argument won.

In retrospect it is clear that the always highly strung Christabel Stafford was having a breakdown. She had some of the looks of Virginia Woolf and maybe she shared her mental instability. The first signs were her falling out with the domestic staff. Our French housekeeper left. Possibly also the matron. It increasingly fell to the boys to do all the domestic housework. GBS was seemingly powerless to stop this slide in the way the school was run. I think my eventually becoming one of her inner circle lay in my being a good listener. Mrs Stafford would read to us and I recall the Heidi books. There was a crucial moment in the story when Heidi had to choose the right road. One indication that I was now in favour was my being one of a privileged group of boys that accompanied her to London to attend an event celebrating the work of the Life Boat Association. So we became her Praetorian guard. I was required to carry out her punishments. Quite what he had done wrong I do not remember, but I had to wipe the face of Lawson (could he have been the future Chancellor?) with a dirty floor cloth. Obviously the school was breaking down and word got out to the parents. There was to be a mass haemorrhaging of boys, school numbers dropping from some 100 to 30. Mrs Stafford disappeared to a nursing home. I suffered a breakdown and recall waking up in the school sanatorium temporarily blinded. Yet Father chose to stay loyal to GBS and so began another extraordinary time at Kingshott. It is just an aspect of being a child that you never question the ways of the adult world and I seem just to have accepted these bizarre events.

At the age of 11 I became head boy. Indeed there seemed to be nothing I did not lead, becoming captain of cricket, football and twice Victor Ludorum of athletics. I was already an opening pace bowler, a good knock at number 7 and a real talent as a slip fielder. I won both sprints but not the 440, a really good hurdler and winner of both the long and high jump. I became more aware of learning. The prospect of taking the Common Entrance examination for Gresham's focussed my mind. Father had put me down at birth for Gresham's and no other school was ever considered. Was I academically bright? The teachers I remember best were Mr Eames for History and George Silver for Divinity. Was I always a natural for History? I've already related how theft lay behind my love of history and all those stolen books from Woolworths were the basis for my illustrating the history we were being taught. Eames could be rather fierce and I was quite often rapped over the knuckles with a ruler. George Silver in time became an important influence in my life, one of the few to worry at my religious development, both as a priest and later as a monk at Nashdom Abbey. Father got on very well with him and there was to be one wonderful holiday, together with another boy from the school, John Eddowes, on the Thames from Marlow to Oxford and back. I was also a natural at Latin and in my final year Mrs Stafford, who had returned, taught us Greek. I rejoiced aloud in speaking Greek verbs and it was a pity Greek played no part in the school curriculum at Gresham's. I did well enough in the Common Entrance exam, came 8th, but was let down by poor maths and did not do well enough to be a scholar.

And what of sexuality? I was still driven by my scoptophilia. In the manner of Keyhole Kate I'd try to espy poor Mr Tate, one of my first teachers, though the keyhole of an upstairs wc. I wonder what the Staffords would have made of such behaviour. How was I aware of Mr Stafford's long willy? Did GBS share our tub after games? We all became rather fascinated by the pubic hairs on an older boy who had presumably returned to do an extra year at the school. I received my one and only sex education lesson when GBS summoned us to explain there was nothing strange in this and that in time we'd be similarly endowed. I recall no abuse at the school unless corporal punishment by cane and ruler constitutes abuse. There was no sex between the boys. I was early on to attract some kudos amongst the boys by describing a couple copulating in the fields I'd seen en route to my convent school. But, wholly privately, I was discovering how to masturbate. I would rub myself pleasurably. But it was not till I was possibly 12 that I had my first ejaculation in the upstairs toilet next to my bedroom at home. At some time the myth that masturbation led to blindness had taken hold. None of this could possibly be discussed with anyone.

It is interesting to compare my personal memories of the school with my school reports. Did they in any way betray that hiatus in the school through Mrs Stafford's illness? GBS's reports are small miracles of characterisation, be they correct or otherwise. There was no reference to my abject misery that first term: 'Anthony has had a very good first term and has made remarkably good progress in so short a time. He is quiet, steady, capable little worker who gives his full attention to what he is doing. He has also fitted in very happily, in spite of initial shyness into all school arrangements, and he should go ahead well next term.' I'm also described improbably as 'a reliable goal-keeper'. Looking ahead to Summer 1945: 'shows an increasingly purposeful application, most good to see in a boy of his age. He has warm sympathies and shows pluck and good sense.' Michaelmas 1945 is more qualified: 'he has plenty of willpower and must use it to tackle the weak spots in his handling of his work. He is delightfully full of interest and sympathy and is a very promising boy.' On Boxing: 'lacks defence'. (No wonder I hated it.) Spring 1946 GBS has a strange report: 'he is an extremely keen worker and player and already sees the general design and goes all out to carry it forward. His character is visibly strengthening'. Equal praise in Summer 1946: 'Anthony brings a splendid spirit of keenness and untiring effort to attain a high standard in all he does in work and play and general activities. He is very capable. His sense of fun and fair play is quite an asset.' On these reports go, Michaelmas 1946: 'Antony is a boy of splendid strength of character, tenacity of purpose and public spirit. It is a great pleasure to watch the straightforward unfolding of character. He carries out his minor duties without fear or favour.' (A reference to my role as enforcer?) Little change for Spring 1947. Summer 1947, I bring 'an excellent spirit of constant effort to bear on work and play and conduct. He is most cooperative and loyal and exerts a splendid influence.' Clearly *esprit de corps* is vital: 'his attitude of loyalty and thoroughness and common sense earns him the well-merited respect of boys and staff alike.'

Another somewhat strange GBS report: 'Anthony is a most conscientious worker and when he realises that we appreciate that fact he will allow himself to continue his effort without cessation. His love of law and order sets a fine example and calls for and gains general respect. At the same time he continues to be a delightfully natural boy.' (Another reference to my joining the Praetorian guard?) GBS writes: 'Many of his mistakes are due to over-conscientiousness. He brings that same conscientiousness to bear on all his duties in the life of the school. He shows plucky determination and loyalty and these qualities leave their mark on others. His dislike of any form of disorder is a great asset. He fully deserves the respect he has won for himself.' In Summer 1948 Anthony 'continues his high principles'.

I must have by now, rather predictably and however prematurely, become head boy. The report for Spring 1949: 'he has consolidated his position as a capable leader'. I was also doing well at work. In Michaelmas 1949 GBS writes: 'he has done much for the school this term by his high standard of conduct and his virility'. (What an odd word to use.) In 1950 GBS writes: 'that he can produce such effort in his work while pulling his full weight with effect in dealing with a somewhat difficult set of contemporaries augurs well for the future. He knows how grateful I am for his straightforward outlook and for his help.' What was that about? Were there difficult boys? Running a school with but 30 boys must have thrown up problems. So to the final report. I like the one on cricket from GBS: 'very useful - a keen and plucky fielder with a sound sense of anticipation. He made himself into a useful fast bowler - must learn to conserve his energy. A delightfully unorthodox bat but he hits the ball hard when he makes contact. As his wrist grows stronger he must concentrate on more orthodox strokes.'

And my final moral report from GBS: 'In spite of the knowledge that he was leaving he never let up in his stalwart and loyal work for the school in general. It is hard to express what we all owe him for the loyalty in difficult times and for his virile encouragement all around him. My wife and I are deeply indebted to him; and I hope he realizes in some measure how wholeheartedly we offer him our most sincere praise and thanks for all he has done for us and for the school. May he ever prosper in all his undertakings.' Here is the first overt reference to the rather dubious role I played in the time of troubles.

It is clear from reports on learning that I was already best at History and English. Music began promisingly then flagged. I had touch on the piano but was a poor sight-reader. I was also good at the classics - Mrs Stafford returned to teach us Greek and Divinity. But French and Maths were weaker.

Kingshott did not drop out of my life on going to Gresham's. It's clear from the diary I kept that I once visited Mr Stafford at the school, that I kept up a correspondence with Mr Eames, and an even more extensive one with George Silver. I realise now it was not till August 1952 that we all went on that boating holiday on the Thames. George may only have two days with us but I recall he and Father coming back one night much the worse for wear. I guess Father befriended George as someone whom he could consult on my growing up. I always thought I'd stayed at the Randolph when we arrived at Oxford wet through but it was at the Royal Oxford. During our stay I visited New, Merton, Christ Church and the Bodleian. Was I always destined for Oxford?

Much later a letter dated 18 August 1966 from Christabel Stafford on the death of GBS from lung cancer. Following x-rays, seeking an explanation of a sharp pain in the lung, 'he suddenly fell to the ground in the hall at Abbey Cottage on his way to making early 8 o'clock tea. It was too pathetic for words to see him smiling, yet unable to recognise anyone.' She had been admitted to a nursing home, Holloway Sanatorium, in Virginia Waters. I must have written to her - I was at UCNW Bangor at the time - and she replied 14 September: 'I can never get over his death after 46 years of companionship. He was working for others to the very last as he did all his life and in spite of various handicaps which increased as he grew older he kept his daily chores and coaching boys going up to the end.' He had broken his left tibia in an accident at Copford Globe (another school?) where he went to work after selling the school. She also had an accident, breaking her thigh. 'I do indeed remember teaching you Greek and your neat scholarly work. Did you go onto Bryanston and what a splendid success you had in an Oxford scholarship! Mr Stafford often spoke of you and he would be proud of you now. I expect he knows all about it. (Was she a spiritualist?) Were you with Eddowes in Greek?' She added: 'I know Bangor University well, having been at a Classical conference there. What lovely surroundings.' I never learnt of her death. One of GBS's most remarkable achievements was in the way he had coped with his headstrong, unstable wife. Under his Headmastership the school returned to its former high standard. I like to think as head boy I played a small part in its recovery.

So was I emotionally damaged by Kingshott? It is clear that I came into line with the school ethos and was seen to be a model schoolboy. Had I surrendered my own identity to the school's *esprit de corps*? But this was clearly a very weird time and I was caught up in a morally corrupted environment. Surely this must have harmed me? The school had hardened me at my separation from family life and the classic process of becoming an emotionally repressed person for later life was well under way. Even so, my sexuality was proving an undertow of rebellion against the norm and may have been the salvation of my keeping, however hidden, some emotional independence. The school certainly laid the foundations of a privileged and first rate education. Might I have been a good classicist? It is hard though to deny that probably I was never to enjoy such a prominent position of authority in all my later life.

Kingshott School

Staff (from left)
Mr Eames, Mr Stafford, Mr Silver

Pupils and staff (Antony back row, 3rd from right)
With Permission of Kingshott School

Antony in Kingshott Sports Day -1948

Antony (centre) in the Little Plays of St Francis – 1949
With Permission of Kingshott School

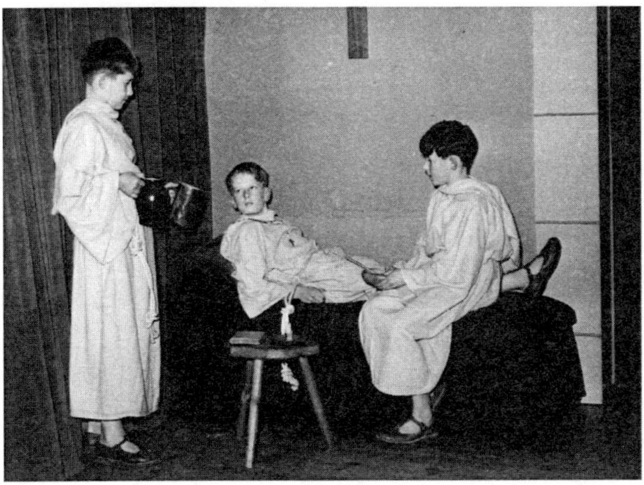

5
GRESHAM'S SCHOOL, HOLT 1950-55

The transition from prep school to public, the rite of passage of most middle class boys, can be traumatic. From being a head boy to beginning all over again as an underdog could have been painful. There was an initial spell of homesickness and I must all over again have cried myself to sleep, but this after all was but another phase in the truly weird life of being a boarder, and I seem to become adjusted fairly quickly. All through life my reaction to new situations is not to look to the past but to buckle down and pursue a policy of survival in the present. To recall those Gresham's years, 1950-55, I have kept by strange chance, diaries - admittedly but brief daily entries - from January 1951 to December 1953, covering the 4th and 5th forms and part of the Lower 6th. I also have my own copies of *The Gresham*, the school's rather impressive termly record of events, and the indispensable source for any history of the school. This has been written by one of its History masters, Steve Benson, entitled *I Will Plant Me a Tree*. Once again, school and family life seemed to be peculiarly separate, yet family life was heading towards the disaster of my parents' divorce.

I lack any record of how I coped with my first term. Did I arrive, as I was usually to do, by train at Holt station via Norwich or did Father drive me with tuck box and all? I was assigned to Old School House, the original 1555 grammar school in Holt itself, a mile away from main school. Twice a day I'd have to walk or bicycle for classes and games. My housemaster, Eric G Kelly, my future key history teacher - and this fact I only learnt through writing this memoir - had only just abandoned bachelordom the summer before to marry Mrs Kelly and to acquire a step-daughter. Initially in the diaries he always features as Old Man. So I found myself in a community of some 100 highly regimented boys, policed by prefects. Junior dormitory was hardly a new experience. Finding myself sharing a study with five others was, however. All new boys were placed on the lowest table in the dining room. I became a fag to head of house, Airs. This was none too burdensome. I'd be assigned such tasks as blancoing his cricket pads. Hitchcock was prefect in charge of our dormitory, keeping a tight control of after-lights behaviour and overseeing our brutally cold morning shower. And maybe I was more miserable than I recall. On returning to school for the Lent term I write, 19 January: 'I felt very miserable as I had to go back to school. Went by train. My tuck box and trunk did not arrive. Wanted to cry.'

In fact there were some crippling aspects to the beginning of my first term. I might well have been bullied. One Sankey, son of a housemaster, threatened to do so, but Heilman came to my rescue. He was one of the glamour boys of the school, to become House captain and Head of school. He was an outstanding athlete. He'd heard of my prowess at games at Kingshott, above all as a sprinter, and decided to take me under his wing. Sankey was frightened off and I was never bullied again. Then there was the nightmare of the collars. Mother misguidedly had bought stiff ones from Rowe's of Bond Street, which I was quite unable to fix, and there were several miserable weeks before soft ones arrived. But the biggest disaster of all was breaking my left arm in my very first game of rugby. I am left-handed. Somehow I coped with my arm in a sling. Having to learn to write with my right hand was a real struggle. Later GBS wrote to my Father 19th December, by way of thanks for the gift of a pen: 'it is good to know that Anthony's arm is now mended though I am very sorry he missed games for the whole term. But with his keenness he will make up for it next term. I do hope it will not interfere with his speed bowling.'

This injury radically altered the way I approached Gresham's. I might well have given preference to games. Now I turned to study, not so much in terms of any pleasure in learning but as an outlet for my competitiveness. The diary shows that I became obsessed about my place in form and the results of termly examinations. The 4th forms were streamed and through my comparatively poor Maths and French I was only in 4b. End of term exam results were posted in the corridor of the main school building and I'd seek these out with morbid concern. I scored highest in Divinity, well enough in History and, interestingly, highly in Biology. Much later I tried to combine History and Biology in the 6th form but the timetable did not permit this. I had some hopes of coming top of class at the end of the year and as the HM read out the order I got ready to get up and collect the form prize, but I came second to Beslay, an older boy but talented: 'rather annoyed but in a way I did not expect to come top.' By the time I entered Form 5H, if still competitive, I was beginning to enjoy education for its own sake.

An entirely different form of competitiveness ran parallel, the making of friends. I don't recall this being paramount at Kingshott. But I kept up a friendship with John Eddowes on leaving, would frequently travel by bus to see him in Barnet during holidays, and I suspect this friendship was indispensable as I floundered in my pursuit of a friend in Old School House. The boy in our entry I sought out was Michael Bloor. He was cleverer than I, a scholar and in 4a. But we messed in the same study. We were both fags for Airs: 'we cleaned his corps things'. (5 June 1951) The diaries show that we did a lot of mucking about together: 'attempted to so some work and write a letter but Bloor and Powley made nuisances of themselves and I was unable to do so.' (8 January) 'Had good fun with Bloor.' (23 February) We both played for the Colts XV in Rugger. Yet it was becoming clear that he was slipping away from me and he had chosen the unprepossessing O'Connell instead as a friend. I made a final bid: 'Did a portrait of Bloor in art.' (17 June 1952) And is it possible Bloor still left open a chance of friendship? There is a truly strange diary entry: 'Had a letter from Bloor, calling himself Thelma. Made Mummy believe he was a girlfriend of mine.' (16 September) And maybe not all was lost: 'Ragged around with Bloor and had an unsuccessful spiritualist meeting.' (1 November) We shared forms in 5H and the lower 6th. He was made a House prefect along with Mackenzie before me. Bloor in fact failed to live up to academic expectation and left school after completing two 'A' levels. It's my understanding he was to take over the family firm of saw makers in Leicester. Only later did I realise why I had lost out to O'Connell.

So I had to make do with other friends. There was the rather slapdash pianist Oldfield who bribed his way into my friendship by bags of reject chocolates. His Father worked for Cadbury's in Norwich. There was the rather wooden Field. In Michaelmas 1952 we shared a study. We were made prefects together though he was later to take precedence. I think he was always destined to be Head of School. I would invite him to join Father on days out at school with the family. He became my official best friend. I was also friendly with Powley and Mackenzie. But another close friend, and this through a breach in school protocol in befriending those from other houses, was Hugh Maddox. Our academic careers were to run parallel and we were groomed together by Kelly for the Oxbridge scholarships. In Michaelmas 1954 he won an Exhibition at Corpus, I but a place at King's. During this Cambridge visit Hugh was influenced by the Evangelicals and in time this contributed to his becoming a priest. I also invited him to join parental outings and he returned the favour by inviting me home. This was to be an eye-opener to me as to how happy family life might be. His parents clearly delighted in each other's company.

Years later, on a holiday in Greece in 1960, I was still haunted by all these quests for friendship. I write in my journal of Heilman and 'his vivid defence' of me from Sankey: 'yet I felt uncertain here - eventually destroyed something which quivered always in the background and made any new beginning impossible.' (Had I sensed a special friendship?) Later Heilman was to warn me off any friendship with Alan Carr, probably the most accomplished mind amongst my contemporaries. 'Bloor's was the friendship I passionately wanted but saw myself giving way to O'Connell. I was hurt. Yet the very slow development of a friendship with Hugh Maddox made up for a considerable amount of misery. He would become a foil to my intellect. But I was never relaxed. I learnt ideas from him but rarely achieved spontaneity. There were those extraordinary evenings we shared together with Hoult Taylor. I was always tongue-tied with embarrassment. My ideas were too "big" for me. Hugh's had a naive but genuine unpretentiousness about them.' I write of 'the terrible friends I had at first, the one who craved my Tarzan books. I felt hemmed in by something sinister. Notice how I changed studies but I didn't resent this exile. Always dreaded being left behind the "bloodies". I was far too unsophisticated to see them as such.' I hated having to share Field with a Platten. (No memory of him.) Why did I form this friendship? Somehow it was never intimate. But I needed it for my prestige. I suppose he had no feminine side to him. I seemed to sum all this up: 'I rarely found a friend who would let me express the side of me that never grew up and my conscientious interest in work.'

Meanwhile in all this abortive search for the ideal friend, family life was breaking down. Family and school were wholly separate spheres. Did I ever foresee the divorce? Once, I must have been about twelve, I caught

Mother and Vivian (Gloster-Downing) kissing beside the tennis court at Elstree Country Club. Intrigued, I called to Georgina also to be a witness. I seem to have read nothing into this. Oddly, I've always quite wrongly believed that Mother left us at the time of my going to Gresham's. In fact it was some two years later, sometime in 1953. The diary gives little away. 'Mummy and Daddy 12th wedding anniversary.' (8 January 1951) 'I had a lovely food parcel and 10/- from Mummy.' (26 March 1951) 'I am home of which I am very pleased.' (3 April 1951) 'I bought Mummy some tulips.' (18 April 1951) 'In the afternoon Mummy took me to see Bob Hope in the Lemon Drop Kid.' (1 May 1951) 'Mummy went out and Lisa very miserable followed and we nearly lost her.' (24 August 1951) Mother had not joined us for our annual Westgate holiday: 'very glad to see Mummy who was much nicer to me.' (17 September 1951) I also registered that Mother did not come down on school trips, sometimes just Father and Georgina, more often Father on his own. Mother and I played cards quite frequently: 'played cards with Mummy. Rummy. She won easily.' (4 January 1952) But then: 'played cards all afternoon and evening with Mummy and Vivian.' (17 January 1952) She's still at home 1 April 1952: 'played cards afternoon with Mummy, won 5 ½. Did some shopping with Mummy but she did not join us for Westgate.' (1 August 1952) 'Went out with Mummy shopping - we went to Edgware and Golders Green. We saw Daddy in the office.' (13 August 1952) But Mother once again does not join us in Westgate. We visit Auntie Betty's flat "which was very beautiful". We'd seen Georgina off for her finishing school in Switzerland. (8

September 1952) On 7 November Mother went to visit Georgina. Lovely present from Mummy with cuff links.' 'Bought Mother's birthday present.' (2 December 1952) There was a happy family Christmas with Granny and Grandpa Pohlman and Uncle Edgar present. I have no diary to refer to after 31st December.

Had Mother tried to prepare me for Vivian as a step-father? Certainly by then I was already referring to his parents as Uncle Tom and Auntie Blanche. Father hated Tom. It was at the Elstree Country Club that Mother used to arrange my piano recitals to a no doubt very embarrassed audience. I played Debussy's Claire de Lune with great touch.

Relationships with Father seem to have been benign. I'd accompany him on his evening walks with Lisa after his return from the office. There were those fishing trips and my ineptness at fly-fishing. It was Father who took us to Rowena Court Hotel in Westgate. He clearly enjoyed his visits to Gresham's as an OG, getting very drunk with Mr Webster, the Art master, at the Feather's hotel. He was generous with presents, new hockey sticks, cricket bats, pocket money. We visited his parents at St Ives and Uncle Bob and Auntie Anne at Hemingford Grey with its attractive bird sanctuary. 'Had a talk with Daddy.' (1 April 1952) What would that have been about? Clearly our best time of bonding was that Thames river trip 16-23 August. Only once do I note Father being cross with me.

So did I really have any idea that my parents were considering divorce? The only clue comes 25th August 1952: 'Mummy and Daddy quarrelled. Went to bed early.'

He did not broach the subject on a school visit 14 November. All those visits by the Pohlmans, however, in December suggest an attempt was being made to patch up the marriage. For me its denouement was played out at school.

By the summer term 1953 the divorce had become inevitable. It was the time of the coronation. There was an additional school coronation holiday 31 May to 3 June. The Gresham reports: 'almost every boy either returned home or else visited one of his friends. One or two, however, lingered at the school in the fond hope that they might lock themselves in the library in imitation of the writers of the Septuagint for a few days. Unfortunately, the attractions of the local festivities proved too strong for them.' I was one of those boys, though have no recollection of joining any local celebration, cannot even recall watching the coronation on TV and must have been exceptional in not celebrating the coronation at all. It must have been at my Father's request that I stayed on in OSH.

In that black box which I inherited from my step-father I discovered this extraordinary letter from Father to Mother, 11 June 1953. It is clear that Mother had left home and disappeared. Father had had to contact Auntie Betty to track her down. She was in fact living in a garden flat in 139 Old Brompton Road, though I was only to visit her there two years later: 'I understand from Betty - I of course have not heard from you - that you have decided to make the break permanent and that your life lies with Vivian.' In fact, as Mother told us years later, that had not been her first intention. She mentioned a man called Mark whom she would rather have married. Then Father continues and I find his concern now very moving.

I am worried about Antony. You can rest assured that whatever the state may be between our respective selves this will make no difference so far as humanly possible to Antony and Georgina. You can see them as and when you like. I would like to encourage this so far as is humanly possible, a continuation of your close interest in them. (This last bit is crossed out.) *Georgina of course is more able to look after herself. With Antony however I shall undoubtedly have difficulties. I have told him nothing about things at the moment. I do not wish to disturb him until after his Exams. As far as I can gather the first lot will be taken this term.* (I was taking 'A' levels after one year.)

If of course your decision is irrevocable then he must be told during the Summer holiday. I should of course be in difficulty with regard to his clothes. Betty mentioned this matter to me and I see no reason why, if you wish, you should not continue to look after this aspect of the case. I also see no reason why you and Antony should not have a holiday together (without Vivian) say at the Rowena Court. I appreciate finances may enter into this and I am quite prepared to pay for the holiday.

You will have noticed that I've continued paying an allowance to you. This I propose to continue for the time being, having in mind that it will be partially used for the children.

Subject to hearing from you as to the finality of your decision and discussing the matter with Antony and Georgina I am prepared to take steps to clear the matter up, so that both the children can visit you freely.

In some ways this was Father's last attempt to rescue the marriage. I believe he still loved Mother though of course he also feared a loss of face as a divorcee. He had a reputation as a good divorce lawyer and put this to good effect in his own case. Exceptionally, for almost always custody went to the mother, he won custody of the children on grounds of Mother's adultery. Mother never took advantage of seeing us, let alone a holiday in Westgate. I was not to see her again till after my Father's second marriage. I have no idea who looked after my clothes. We had a series of disastrous housekeepers, either alcoholics or suicides, or both. Nor do I recall precisely when I was told about the divorce, not, I think, when Father next visited for Speech day or Old Boy's day. I do recall Kelly telling me in his smoky study, so maybe I learnt it from him. Father was quite wrong about Georgina. Maybe with her Electra complex she had won Father for herself, but her lurking hysteria in time became a real problem. With my reverse Oedipus complex I also took it in my stride but Father could have had no idea of the problems it would lead to in the short run or the long. Both Georgina and I were very badly damaged. Would we have been less so if they had divorced earlier? They left it till late on so as to give us a normal childhood and to spare us pain.

It is shocking that we still do not have a No Fault or No Blame divorce. Later I researched divorce reform in Britain and France, though only published my findings on France.

A rather puzzling aspect of my early years was indifferent health. I spent a good deal of time in the school san with flu or earache. I often complained of stomach ache and this at the time was put down to growing pains. In fact it was a grumbling appendix and it was only after leaving school that it was operated on: it was close to bursting. I suppose I was growing quite fast. The diary records: 10 May 1951, 7 stone 13, 5ft 5; 8 May 1952, 9st 1, 5ft 8. My battle with the school matron, Miss Gooch did not help: 'as usual the Gooch was in a bad mood with me. I hate her like poison.' (31 May 1951) Maybe I exasperated her with my untidiness, firstly those collars, then my hair. Did I have a double crown? I recall Airs in an end of year speech as House captain in 1951 describing, as if in a dream, all the boys passing before him, and spoke of Copley 'with hair like yellow straw'. As I became more senior Gooch and I became reconciled. I was in fact growing into a tall and willowy boy, with some of the good looks of a Rupert Brooke.

The school paid great attention to sport. This had not been the case under its first two headmasters, Howson and Eccles and they had ignored inter-school house matches. But this had all changed, and under Martin J Olivier the ideal boy - whatever his academic prowess - had to be a good athlete. For better or worse, subsequent feelings of self-esteem are often dependent on being good at games at school, and for those who were ill adapted to sport, this becomes a painful memory. I had been a good games player at Kingshott and was no doubt expected to do well at Gresham's. I certainly took games seriously and for years subscribed to sports magazines. I was in all the House teams. One of most treasured memories is scoring a try from my own 25 in a Junior House match. I may have been in all the Colts teams but only went on to be in the 2nd XV for Rugby and the 2nd XI for Hockey. But I was good at cricket. My best year was 1953-4 when I was awarded my school colours. I was a medium pace opening bowler with an ability to swing the ball. The coach, Mr Thomas, rated me as good as Andrew Corran, who went on to be a county player. Culling reports from the Gresham: 'I suffered from being bowled too long' against Felsted, though took 3 for 4; 'added pace and dignity to the proceedings against the Masters, taking 4 for 21'; 'seemingly miraculously caught and bowled Hodgkin' in the match against the MCC and I can still feel the sting in my hand. I had a long arm and was a useful fielder in the deep as well as being a good slip catcher. Next year I tried to bowl too fast and was dropped, but then everything fell apart in all kinds of ways.

But my real passion was for Athletics. As a junior in 1953 I won the Hurdles and, had the stop clock been functioning, I suspect I would have set a record that would have lasted for years. I won the Long jump with 18ft 10 ½, the high jump, the javelin, 126 feet 4, but only 2nd in the 100 yards. In the seniors in 1954, I came 3rd in the 100 yards, only 3rd in the hurdles (my legs were not long enough for the high hurdles), 2nd in the long jump (Andrew Mulligan, a future Rugby international for Ireland, won), and 2nd in the javelin. I got my colours through representing the school in three events in the annual match against Norwich Grammar School, in the long jump, second again to Mulligan and just short of 20 foot, in the javelin and in the school 4x100 relay. My long arm made me a natural for the javelin and in practice could throw nearly 200 feet, but was seriously restricted by the rules of competition. My obsession was the long jump. One of my favourite books was a history of the Olympic Games and I nurtured the ambition of representing GB in that event. I would spend hours practising, both at school and on the beach at Westgate. I routinely cleared 20ft in practice.

On a higher plane was drama. I came late to house plays. I had already been deeply moved by Jeremy Tunstall's performance of Stanhope in *Journey's End.* I turned up for an audition of *The Doctor's Dilemma* and found myself unexpectedly cast as the tubercular Louis Dubedat. My diary goes on about learning my lines. I got a mixed review in the Gresham: 'Louis Dubedat was both a scoundrel and a man of considerable charm. A R Copley brought out the former without ever quite convincing us of the latter, but whether this was his fault or the dramatist's was not altogether clear.' (March 1953 p36) But my next role was a gem, the false Inspector-General, Ivan Ivanovitch Khlestikov, in Gogol's *The Inspector General.* Bloor played my servant, Osip, so maybe the friendship still carried on, if only on stage. We enjoyed a very good review: 'here were two beautiful performances, their part forming such a vital element of the plot of mistaken identity. The one was cowardly and suave to a superbly unpleasant degree, the other, both in appearance and manner, quite excellently portrayed what our uninformed imaginations pictures the hard-headed Russian peasant stock to be.' (March 1954 p131)

I made but one appearance in a school play as Eros, Mark Antony's servant, in Antony and Cleopatra. This was in the Open air theatre in the woods. Here I was in brilliant company, John Tusa as Antony, Alan Carr as Enobarbus. Eros draws a sword on himself rather than carrying out Antony's order to kill him: I managed 'the tragical (sic) self-sacrifice of Eros quite perfectly.' (The Gresham July 1953 p69) Alan Carr was the most gifted actor of his generation at school, with a memorable Feste already behind him. Despite Heilman's warning, we did become friends and he was to introduce me to the London theatre. This was currently dominated by Eliot's and C B Fry's verse drama and this had the fatal consequence of my trying to write verse drama.

Both house and school plays were produced by Hoult Taylor, far and away the most gifted member of the school's staff. I never relaxed in his company but his influence over me was huge.

From the beginning of the school the CCF, at one point renamed the Officer Training Corps, had featured prominently. I think Tony Britten was absolutely right to speculate in his film that its intrusive presence turned schoolboy Benjamin Britten into a pacifist. I only joined in my second year. Thereafter I'm now astonished at the degree to which the CCF took over school life with three sessions a week. To quote a few diary entries: 'at first we formed and marched. Practised a few things and we were shown parts of a rifle. Pretty heavy things to carry around.' (28 September 1951) 'In corps we practised drill. I had to go out and demonstrate a halt.' There were field days:

'started off at 9am on bike. We had a rifle and in all I fired 5 blanks. First we defended a kind of house and in the afternoon a hill. Mainly we just sat around, watched them encircle us. Wonderful lunch. Great hunks of bread and cheese.' (9 October 1952) This was at Weybourne. All this was in aid of being instructed for Certificate A. But the true aim was of course preparing us for National Service, a prospect that hung over all our school days. One old boy wrote to the Gresham 'that the high standard of training had been inestimable value to them and it was therefore imperative that this should be mentioned.' (The Gresham December 1951 p79) J B Tunstall (a elder brother?) came back from Korea to give us a lecture on the Korean war: all about 'weapons, food, clothing and a comparison of Chinese, American and British tactics.' (March 1952 p113) I am amazed at the way I, one of the least technological of people, went on to be a Sergeant in Weapons instruction and could expertly strip and reassemble a Bren gun. Somewhat weirdly, one OG wrote in and anticipated my own naval National Service on HMS Ocean and HMS Forth, 'a converted Cunarder from the time of the slump and now a submarine depot ship.' (March 1954 p143) I was indeed to follow Leakey's advice and join the Navy. (March 1954 p144) I hoped this way to avoid all the mindless drill of the Army.

CCF camp at Otley in 1953 was memorable for wholly non-military reasons. It was a camp described in the Gresham as 'notable for its sanity and sanitation' with Butlin's holiday camp features, 'extreme comfort and luxury' were described. But I recall its downside: 'it is true that having spent two hours and much energy digging trenches through thick clay, we were not enraptured to receive orders to destroy all traces of our handiwork at once.' (9 December 1953 p106) But I have far more personal memories. I recall being covered in soot the moment I stepped out of the train at Leeds. We were in urgent need of the Clean Air act. Lying on my palliasse in our supposedly luxury tents I had a kind of mystical experience, a calling by Christ to dedicate my life to being a missionary and be ready to court martyrdom in the struggle against apartheid. Had I already read T S Eliot's *The Cocktail Party* in which Celia's vocation as a missionary in Africa ends with her being crucified upside down on an ant-hill? It was a vocation that haunted me for years.

We were in fact being indoctrinated into the Cold War. At my first School Speech Day the Chairman of Governors declared: 'I have no fear of the result if we are driven to a shooting war. But I think we have got to remember that our way of life is under attack in the Cold war.' Oddly, he put his faith in friendship, 'one of the great principles of Public School life.' Air Vice Marshal Sir Hugh Walmsley, our visiting speaker, began by reminding us National Service had, because of the Korean war, been extended to two years: 'I would say quite definitely that it should be the duty of every Public School boy, whether in the Navy, the Army, or the Air Force, to make it his aim to obtain Commissioned rank. You should not be a shirker.' (July 1951 p48) Another indoctrination was in the Commonwealth. One Sir Ronald Weeks in 1952 rhapsodised: 'the British strength lies in the Empire, or as some people call it, the British Commonwealth. A united British Empire with its statesmen working in harmony, with its population redistributed to develop its natural resources could produce a society which would be a greater power in maintaining peace than any other single factor that I know of.' (July 1952 p136) Much later Harry Pitt, my History tutor at Worcester, saw us as a lost generation, programmed to rule an Empire that was disappearing.

And all this was beginning to rub off on me. My political awakening came with reading the Daily Express, available in the OSH games building, following with morbid fascination the way the Chinese Communists were pushing down into the Korean peninsula and the slow reverse by the UN. I was not really aware of the strong left wing tradition in the school's history, Erskine Childers, Tom Wintringham, W H Auden, Stephen Spender and was there indeed a school D notice on Donald Macleans' defection? Yet I do recall my being very aware of his name on the Schools Honour Board.

And there was a provocative reminder of how close Cold War be. One day a rather drunk American airman from one of the nearby B Bomber bases wandered into the grounds of OSH and some boys enjoyed an electrifying conversation with him in the same games room. For me this was an erotic encounter. Kelly was very disapproving.

In my years at Gresham's it was at its lowest point in its history, only matched by the appalling loss of its boys during the First World War. First there was a serious breakdown in its moral order and secondly, largely prompted by the way this was mishandled, a crisis in its governance. Here was yet another Kingshott-like experience, though this time I was a bystander and to an extent a victim. In matters disciplinary, the school could not have been more different than under its first two headmasters. In its Honour code, already mentioned, boys took an oath not to swear, not to smoke, and not to indulge in any indecency. They were required to report anyone who broke the code. J H Simpson in his biography of Howson put it this way: 'there must be a definite compact, an understanding between master and boy, binding the boy not only - or perhaps I should say, not so much - to refrain from the offences in question.' (*Howson of Holt* p62) Auden had seen this as totalitarian. Britten did not believe it worked in practice. Of his time he wrote: 'I think then the Honour's system was a positive fiction. If Eccles knew what happens he would either disbelieve it or have 10 blue fits. It is no good trying an honour system on boys who have no honour. Boys small or rather weak are turned into sour or bitter boys and ruined for life.' (Quoted in Kildea's Biography p51) But it was the same system that saw the ending under Eccles of all corporal punishment. Several masters, including Kelly, Hoult Taylor, A B Douglas and Max Parsons had been appointed during this regime, so possibly it still had some hold on the school. But Benson writes 'the honour system had outlived its somewhat ambivalent ethical code by the 1930s.' (p33) Even so, he makes claims for it: Gresham's was seen as 'a remarkably happy and friendly place. Bullying was extraordinarily rare and homosexuality likewise.' It was a school free of scandal. 'The promise not to indulge in any form of indecency appears to have meant something to the boys of Gresham's.' (Benson p41)

All this was radically different under the headmastership of Martin J Olivier, appointed, it would seem, without a proper advertisement of the post in 1944. The Governors saw fit to make a speedy appointment, the better to manage the return from Newquay to a school substantially damaged by the Army's occupation. Olivier was an effective administrator, pulled off the return well and soon school numbers rose dramatically. But the moral climate of the school had wholly changed. The Honour code gave way to one of not being found out. Olivier reintroduced the cane. I believe Max Parsons, a rather eccentric Latin teacher, did believe at Woodlands in open access between boy and housemaster. I'm not so sure Kelly did, puffing away on his pipe in his study. I'd fallen out with him over a breach in the bicycle rules. It was claimed I'd run down some lady on the cycle track. In my diary I write: 'I may have done it but I don't think I did. Didn't feel a thing.' (14 February 1952.) Even so, I had to apologise and was put off bikes for a week. All this was at the time of the King's funeral.

But then there was a far more serious incident. I'd ridden out of the cycle track by the school library onto the road and collided with a car. I was indisputably to blame. Miraculously I was only badly bruised but had to go to the school san. The owner of the car claimed it was a write-off and I don't know how Father settled the insurance claim. Olivier waited till I'd left the san before summoning the entire school outside the chapel: 'Trish told the whole school about a bicycle accident and quite how annoyed he was.' (Diary 16 July 1952) Relationships with Kelly were mended when I got my school colours for cricket, and he made me a sub-prefect. Apart from Olivier sanctioning my taking my 'O' levels ahead of being 16, I was not otherwise on his radar screen. But his histrionic behaviour was becoming ever more apparent, evidenced in his obsessive practice of our entering and leaving chapel in an orderly fashion.

But an altogether more serious breakdown in the moral order was about to break over the school in Michaelmas 1953. Benson makes no mention of this. Homosexuality had spread throughout the 4th and 5th forms of the school. Usually it exhibits itself in relationships, often platonic, between older and younger boys, but on this occasion it seems only to have been rampant among the younger boys. I have no idea how this came about beyond the fact that homosexuality is rife in single sex boarding schools. Olivier was wholly ill-equipped to deal with this crisis. He resorted to mass beatings of all those detected, keeping a note book, I was told much later, of all those he'd beaten. All this has the feel of an exercise in mass sadism. He may have taken time out to marry the gym mistress at nearby Runton School. But he was obviously besotted with his House and School captain, I M Petersen, and his sexual preferences were barely controlled. I was myself wholly unaware of this rampant sexuality going on all around me.

This was the beginnings a breakdown in respect for Olivier which led to the next big crisis, his enforced resignation. I did wonder in retrospect if he was already exhibiting signs of the illness that was to kill him quite soon after leaving the school.

He held odd and contradictory views on education. His ideas were expressed in those annual addresses at Speech Day. He told us not take hobbies seriously and to avoid a career in architecture, journalism, diplomacy, the stage and films. In 1952 he sought a *via media* between cranky teaching by eccentric school teachers and a more overtly conventional approach: 'I hope that we have originality without wild excesses, coupled with respect for well-tried methods.' (The Gresham, July 1952 p31) In 1953 he attacked High Master Dr Eric James of Manchester Grammar School for his emphasis on academically brilliant boys in favour those who also excelled at games: 'these boys are better all-round human beings and they are the nation's most precious asset.' But then he swung the other way and argued it 'was equally important that the rest should be educated to take a worthy place.' Indeed, he seemed to be saying, you can have enough of brilliant boys. (The Gresham, July 1953 pp61-2) Maybe he summed it all in 1954: 'our chief task in Public school is character training and training for adult life. But character training must not be an excuse for bad training in the class room.' (The Gresham, July 1954 p16) Whether or not all this added up to any coherent theory of education, it did not save him from the crisis he faced.

I was always an outsider in the crisis of Olivier's headmastership. Here was my second experience of a school environment corrupted from the top. Who knows the full story? Possibly John Tusa, a school prefect at the time. It was brought to a head when all the school prefects independently went to Fishmongers Hall to tell the School Governors they had lost respect for him as a person and faith in his leadership. (Or so I assume.) Heilman was then School Captain and he certainly would have despised Olivier's fawning attentions on his senior boys. Clearly the Governors had to react to this extraordinary protest. Was Olivier given the option of resignation over being sacked? He fought to stay on. One manoeuvre he made was to try and win over OG's and he approached my Father with the bribe that were he to support him he would make me a School prefect. Father for once did not support the authorities and so I was not. In a minor way I was a victim of the crisis. Olivier saw out my own time at Gresham's and indeed played a crucial part in my academic future.

I'd now embarked on the one justification for public school privilege, its 6th form education and in my case preparation for the Oxbridge scholarship. There was always an inherent tension between its *dirigisme* and its encouragement of independent thought. Yet at no later stage was I ever to receive such a close monitoring of my work. From its beginnings in 1900 Gresham's was unusual in rejecting a Classics sixth in favour of a modern syllabus, the Natural Sciences, Modern Languages, History and English. I would have been a good classicist, winning the Hambro Latin prose prize in 1953 by following Parson's advice of drastically over-simplifying the translation into Latin. Indeed, I've always suspected here was a lasting influence on my style, the tendency to pare down. I would have welcomed a 6th form education that straddled Science and the Humanities and favoured combining Biology and History. And if I was always poor at Arithmetic I was actually perfectly strong at Algebra and Geometry and a science education was on the cards. But it was to be

History and English I turned to, always my strongest subjects since Kingshott. I made a fatal mistake in choosing the soft option of History with Foreign Texts over Economics.

So my future was now entrusted to Eric Kelly and Hoult Taylor. Both had joined the school in 1928 and became very close friends. Kelly, an Oxford 1st, was a very thorough teacher, dictated notes, and over time I had some 30 notebooks of his teaching, a kind of Kelly version of Edwards' notes. He has been described as 'quietly spoken, unruffled, modest, with a dry sense of humour and a twinkle in his eye.' Did I have a genuine vocation for History? I can recall reading with difficulty Wingfield Stratford's *King Charles the Martyr,* my rather odd choice of book from my reading prize in my first year. I seem to have been excited by the Reformation and Napoleon in the lower forms but the breakthrough came with Walizewski's biography of Peter the Great. Kelly at first saw my essays as still 'O'-levellish, but it was he who insisted on mastering the facts. In his report for Michaelmas 1952 he wrote: 'he has done some good work and should develop well. If he reads widely and follows the method of work suggested he should do well.' For Lent he thought I might well get an 'A' level in one year, as indeed I did. The Summer report read: 'he has worked very well and with seriousness. However he is young and has to learn to consolidate and widen the scope of his knowledge.' Now we move into a new mode, looking for an 'S' level and anticipating Oxbridge: 'has made a start with general historical reading. This branch of work needs careful attention of anyone who hopes for a university scholarship.' (Michaelmas 1953) By

Lent 1954: 'he has industry and some ability. His written work needs firmer treatment, but he is gradually getting a better idea of what is wanted. He should put up a good performance in June.' In fact it was not to be. I only got an A level again. Still, Kelly continued to be hopeful: 'if he concentrates chiefly on his general historical subjects and follows the suggestions made, he should make a good impression in his examinations in December.' All this has a *dirigiste* feel to me.

Hoult Taylor taught in a wholly different way. There was much I did not know about him at the time. He had in fact been appointed to teach music and indeed taught Britten. Taylor then gave regular piano recitals but Britten was not enthusiastic: 'Mr T was very courageous but that's all.' I don't seem myself to have been appreciative: of one Hoult Taylor school concerts I only write: 'quite good.' (Diary 29 February 1952) But his real talent was as producer of school and house plays. Indeed he left the school during the war to take up an appointment in drama at the BBC. Peter Brook wrote of his admiration for Taylor: 'an exciting outsider who could be wickedly indiscreet. The greatest privilege was to be invited by him to tea.' (Quoted Benson pp88-9) He dressed flamboyantly at the time for the 1930s, inviting some ribaldry from the boys. I do remember some colourful waistcoats but otherwise sober tweed suits. He gave us minimal notes. Class work took the form of reading out texts aloud and expressing our response. Here was the beginning of self-discovery. Hoult Taylor's reports were rather bland: 'he has continued to work both intelligently and well.' (Lent 1953) Rather more friendly: 'he has worked extraordinarily well and written some good essays. Further experience should give him the necessary maturity of style.' (Summer 1953) For Summer 1954: 'his work has been exceedingly painstaking and conscientious. I hope he obtains the success he deserves.' And I was to get an 'S' level.

Summer 1954 was an *annus mirabilis* in terms of school prizes. I won the A C Benson Essay prize, a three hour essay on a single topic e.g. Fashion, Toleration, and an indicator of how well one could deal with the Oxbridge examination. I shared the J H Simpson History prize with Hugh Maddox. And it was conceded by Hoult Taylor, when Frears and I read out our prize essays, I should have won outright, rather than shared, the Christopher Brown Memorial prize in English. I'd even got a writing and art prize the year before, much to the chagrin of my contemporaries. My hand writing was very poor. Yet I had ploughed History with Foreign Texts, had only been awarded a County scholarship, and clearly all was to be played for with the Oxbridge scholarships.

But was I to try for History or English? Kelly had just achieved outstanding Cambridge scholarships for John Tusa and Alan Carr at Trinity and King's. But he wanted more. It seems that Hoult Taylor, recognising how keen his old friend Kelly was for more awards before he retired, graciously gave way.

So I embarked on a reading programme which opened up extraordinary new vistas. Some of these had been anticipated in my reading for 'A' level English, J S Mill's essay *On Liberty* and the poetry of Shelley. But now I found myself pondering such issues as natural rights and the role of punishment. A key text was J B Bury's *The Idea of Progress.* Kelly had carefully annotated D C Somervell's abridged version of Toynbee's massive work on History and Comparative Civilisation. But I was beginning to read independently. A writer to leave a lasting influence was John McMurray. I've never thought any differently since on the necessary connection between freedom and equality. I was engaging in a debate between Communism and Christianity. But then by mischance I alighted on the writing on the nature of History by the Russian mystic, Nicholas Berdyaev, and this had a disastrous impact on my thinking. And so I sat in December 1954 the scholarship examination for King's, the only college I'd ever considered.

It is presumed that public school boys are far better equipped for the kind of conversations that these scholarships require. In fact I was pretty much tongue-tied when I was given tea by the college's Senior Tutor, L P Wilkinson and quite unable to respond to his discussion of the SCR's new décor. Far worse was to be my viva. I found myself floundering as I tried to explain the ideas of Berdyaev. My examiners were kind enough to say I had reached Exhibition standard but felt I was going in the wrong direction. There was an alarming moment when it seemed I had not even won a place and would have to sit again, but Olivier sorted this out on my behalf. King's were happy for me to come up the following October. Would that have been my best long term bet? In fact I think not. I would have been dwarfed by cleverer contemporaries at King's and sunk without trace.

It was Olivier who decided I should try instead for the Open Fletcher Scholarship at Worcester College in March. I have no recollection of how I prepared for this. But I was sick at the time and was to take the examination in the house san with Mrs Kelly my invigilator. This of course took a lot of stress off me and may account for my success. I was told of the award before visiting the college. And all I can recall of this was an exchange near the Porter's lodge with Harry Pitt when I replied to some enquiry that I preferred Buxtehude to Bach. I hope this convinced him the college had made the right choice.

At this point I should have left. I could have gone abroad to learn another language. Learnt how to drive. But Father once again put on his authority hat and I returned. It was a disastrous term. My body seemed to have packed up and I played little cricket and did not enter for the athletics. Still, I was house champion at tennis. Academically I was stale. Foolishly I competed for the Benson prize again but lost out to Graham Howes. He went on to a far more prestigious academic career at Cambridge, if less productive. Together we were to co-edit the 1955 *Grasshopper*, celebrating the school's quartercentenary and this involved a rewarding correspondence with the school's greats, Lord Reith, Auden, Britten, Spender. I tried to take up the violin but could not focus on the strings, a squint that was only corrected years later. Much of my time I just went for long bicycle rides in the beautiful North Norfolk landscape. I was beginning to take myself seriously as a poet. I was awarded the Fordham Serious Verse prize, though I suspect that was a consolation prize from Hoult Taylor. I was miserable as a prefect. Kelly had never recovered from the sexual scandal and became paranoid about discipline. I hated the role of disciplinarian he insisted on. Just as well I was not appointed a school prefect. Kelly was to give me a poor last report, one which I feared would sink my chances of a commission in the Navy. Yet there was a positive outcome. I was becoming de-institutionalized and seeing through the flawed system of the public school. In fact I was probably going through more than a reaction from three and half years of sustained academic effort and having a kind of breakdown. There was still an unresolved crisis of sexuality. Oddly, it was to be National Service that was to drag me from this emotional turmoil.

It has been impossible to trace copyright holders of all official school photos.

School – 1951
Antony (front row, 4th from right). Bloor (front row, 3rd from right)

School – 1954
Mr Kelly (centre). Antony (3rd row, 3rd from left)

Gresham's School – Old School House

Gresham's School Chapel

Antony in Long Jump

Antony collecting prize – 1954

Antony (front centre)

Antony (2nd from right) as 'Eros' in Antony & Cleopatra – 1954

Antony (Centre) in The Inspector General with Bloor (his servant) on the right

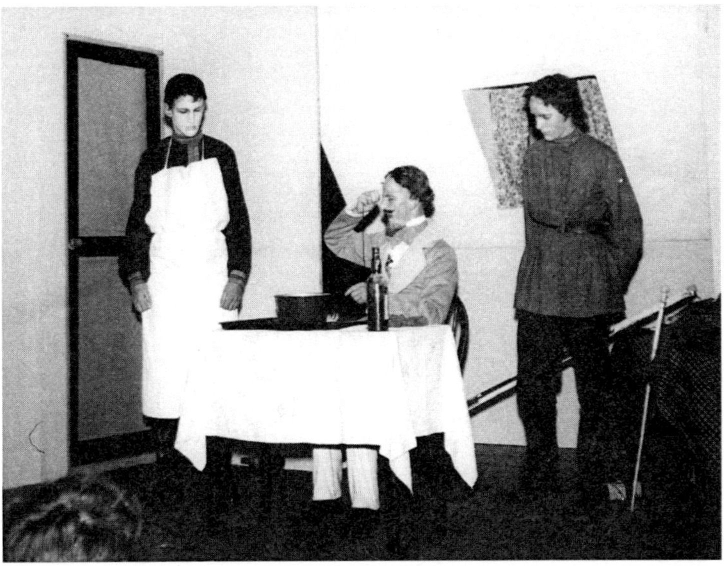

6
A NAVAL NATIONAL SERVICE 1955-57

I wrote this account before embarking on the autobiography. It was prompted by several discussions with Richard Vinen, researching the whole history of National Service and in whose book I was indeed to feature quite prominently. The second was an invitation by the Master of Rutherford College, University of Kent, to give a so-called Grass Roots lecture on my experience of National Service. This encouraged more organised thoughts on the matter. For the meeting with Richard Vinen in 2013 I typed out all those passages from official journals and private diaries which I thought would interest him the most, mainly those on basic training, the Cyprus Emergency and Suez. I should explain that all trainee officers, Upper Yardsmen in NS terminology, and midshipmen thereafter had to submit an official journal, and that I had started keeping a private diary between leaving school and joining up. However embarrassing they be, I have allowed these diaries on grounds of authenticity to speak for themselves, without recourse to much retrospective comment. I am aware that the chapter will be rather teasing, for it raises many contentious questions but only addresses these obliquely, but that is in the nature of such a personal witness statement on major historical events. I'd reread for my talk Trevor Royle's *The Best Years of Their Lives: The National Service Experience 1945-63*, published back in 1986 and designed to coincide with an Exhibition at the Imperial War Museum on National Service. My Official Journal as an Upper Yardsman was one exhibit in that exhibition.

Almost certainly there has been much subsequent literature on the subject. National Service had in a sense merely been carried over from the war but was formally introduced in the National Service Bill of March 1947. The length of service yo-yoed between 18 months, one year, back to 18 month and then after the Korean War up to two years, with various periods in the reserve - three and a half after the Korean war. However at the time I joined up in October 1955 it was already critically under review. Increasingly the Armed forces preferred a regular and more professional army and public opinion was turning against it. In 1949 57% favoured, 33% opposed; by 1953 these figures were reversed. In 1957 Duncan Sandys' white paper planned to phase it out by 1962, though manpower shortages saw it spilling over into 1963. I can recall being summoned to the quarter deck on HMS Vanguard on completion of my NSUY training and being told by the Captain that NS men were now superfluous to requirement. What a way to begin one's new role as a midshipman.

Rather perversely, I thought, Richard Vinen seemed little interested in my personal experience of the Cyprus Emergency and Suez - no doubt he had already seen too many of the same - but wanted to know what my political attitudes were at the time, how I might have voted, and then the social values I brought to bear, and lastly, what indeed the whole experience of NS had meant to me in the long run. I'll return to that at the end. Of course I could not vote till I was 21. My political outlook was an amalgam of values I had acquired through my study, above all of English literature, at school. I was much under the influence of Shelley and his anarchism, J S Mill's essay *On Liberty* (indeed no text has probably done more to shape my political outlook - I wonder what Maurice Cowling would have made of that), the Christian Socialist values of John McMurray (though these I encountered in preparation for my Oxbridge scholarship examinations), plus a rather vulgar Marxism, but then fatally I encountered the Thirties poets, Auden and Spender. Spender became a role model and I was convinced I was to be a poet - well I won the School Serious Verse prize. I fear this was to have a fatally florid effect on my various writings. How embarrassed we are by the *personae* of our past. Indeed, looking back across a chasm of 50 years one cannot always recognize oneself.

This heady brew was always going to be source of conflict with a Navy steeped in a Cold War ideology. Royle makes the point: 'quite simply it was rarely advisable for any NS to express his political leanings especially if they were to the left.' (p241) In my private diary there is a long debate between a Christian and a Communist in which the Christian concedes that in the long run in a materialist age Communism was bound to prevail. In a way I was a natural participant in this Cold War debate. Such were the requirements of writing the official journal that I was probably to become more engaged with contemporary affairs than at any other time of my life. Socially, product of a professional family background and public school, I was genuinely concerned as to how I would fare in the social environment of the lower deck. As a devotee of Spender's *World within World* in fact I longed to cross these class frontiers. My fear was that I would be rejected.

There were two decisions I had to make about NS, which service and when to enlist. So why the Navy? I took no pleasure in mucking about in small boats. Possibly it was for family reasons. I had recently acquired a step-mother who had been a WREN officer and was then a senior officer in the RNVR[1]. My Father had entertained naval ambitions before becoming a solicitor. In fact I suspect the real reason was my perception that anything had to be better than the Army. When, was easier to decide. The choice was between straight from school or after University. All the evidence shows that graduates adjusted far less well to forces' discipline than those straight from school. My college, Worcester College, strongly encouraged my getting it out of the way. It never seems to have crossed my mind to be a conscientious objector. Some 0.4% of NS recruits were, quite a few of whom ended up serving six months in prison. To join the Navy, a minority choice, you had to have joined the RNVR and yet I have a curious blank in my memory about this experience. I do recall spending evenings for training on board HMS President, then moored alongside the Embankment. My medical, 14 September 1955, prompted

[1] RNVR = Royal Naval Volunteer Reserve

this curdling reflection: 'I came for the first time into close contact with members of another class. Possibly they were coarse, but openly and naturally so, as against the surface nicety of certain people in society and I found a strange freshness in talking to them.' I also recall real anxiety at having scorched my bell-bottoms, trying to make creases, but I need not have worried. On joining up October in Victoria barracks, Southsea, Portsmouth I handed in my old gear without there being any comment and a new set was issued. So I began my basic training.

Basic Training

In fact basic training, just a fortnight of mainly drill, was a mild affair compared to the Army. Maybe the Navy always recognised that you were going to get the best out of sailors if they were left to show initiative: the Army still seemed bent on turning its raw recruits into cannon fodder. Certainly, a few were to be driven to suicide by its mindless discipline. Of course those from boarding school adjusted far more easily to barrack room communal living than those straight from home. A charming PO was in charge of our entry. There was an unpleasant PO Harris; but we, in our sophisticated way, put this down to domestic troubles. I think at this early stage I realised that the Armed Forces are run by their NCO's. The officers are just the top dressing though they take both the credit and the blame. So almost immediately I was faced with the option of going for OT. I guess the fatal competitiveness indoctrinated by public school led me to enter. Was this a mistake? Certainly it was a free choice. It consisted of a number of verbal challenges at which I was naturally good and practical challenges in which I must have passed muster. Anyway I was selected for the Upper Yardsmen course.

At this point one should have been posted to one or other of the two Aircraft Carriers, HMS Theseus and HMS Ocean, the training ships, but both were at sea. So began an exceptional period on the lower deck for Upper Yardsmen. The event I recall most vividly whilst still at Victoria Barracks was the visit of Khrushchev and Bulganin and two Russian cruisers to Portsmouth. I record in the private diary on espying the Russian sailors at a NAAFI dance being fired by a desire for international peace. We formally visited the ships and I was very touched to be propositioned by a Russian rating. Meanwhile, underneath the ship, Commander Crabb was getting himself blown up.

To kill time we were then dispatched to HMS Devonport and in my case to a frigate then in dry dock, HMS Leeds Castle. Just as well, too, for I was always seriously seasick the few occasions we did exercises in the English Channel. In time, though, I acquired my sea legs, crossing the notorious Bay of Biscay without distress. So began this rather anomalous spell on the lower deck but as officers to be. It could have been akin to policemen finding themselves among prisoners. But solidarity is all on the lower deck and we were somehow assimilated. In the diary I record: 'I am now living in the most crowded and cramped surroundings I have as yet had to survive. The men are comparatively friendly, although am by no means one of them, possibly I am not meant to be.' Whatever skills I went on to acquire in domestic hygiene - mess inspection was a religious ritual - and cooking were initiated here. I learnt to sling a hammock and found them very comfortable. We wasted a great deal of time chipping paint off the outside of the ship. Learning to waste time was one of the regrettable lessons of NS. Much later I was to spend hours pootering about the quarterdeck as OOW[2] on board the shore-based HMS Forth: my main task was to spot and salute admirals passing by in their barges. Skiving was the word for getting out of work. Did I really write in my diary: 'I must confess pleasure at being an NSUY and I felt pleasantly conspicuous as I walked through Weymouth being the sole person with a white hat-band.'

Yet the situation was Kafkaesque. We were under observation. On joining Leeds Castle the Captain, Lt Commander MacDonald, told us what a privileged position we were in - and here I quote from my official journal: 'we can meet the real men of the lower deck and by being with them grow to understand and appreciate their thoughts and feelings. This would be of great benefit if we should later become officers as we should be able to know where we stood with the men under us, know what the men expected of us as officers and because a spirit of understanding helps to produce fairness and happiness.' The Captain reminded us of the standards we must uphold as Upper Yardsmen: 'we as potential officers have the prestige of officers as our responsibility.' Later the Captain gave us a bizarre lecture on the nature of leadership, with

---

[2] OOW = Officer of the Watch

negative role models in Charles XII, Napoleon and Hitler, positive in General Wolfe and Nelson. Frederick the Great set too tough a standard of discipline. Christ, through his moral example, was seen as the greatest leader. 'The quality of leadership', to quote, 'is one that embraces many qualities, qualities such as loyalty, unselfishness, ability, obedience, pride in oneself, one's ship, one's country. These qualities can best be produced by the personal example of the leader. Inspiring good morale is a high requirement.' On a more mundane level, 'this necessitates good organisation, seeing that the food is good and that the mail is well organised, which is especially important in wartime'. The Captain concluded: 'the qualities of a leader are many and demanding but they are qualities that can be developed.' Here was quite some moral baggage to take with us on joining HMS Ocean for formal NSUY training.

So began a 16 week Upper Yardsman course on HMS Ocean - seen as superior to HMS Theseus through its being less *dirigiste* in its approach - eventually transferring to the shore-based HMS Vanguard. For me the most exciting days were those of a visit to Franco's Spain. I like to think I saw the germs of a new Spain: to quote from the official journal (but the same entry was made in the private): 'however much Spain may have tried to retreat into her shell post Civil War, new influences must have profoundly affected the entire structure of Spanish life. Spain has commitments in Spanish Morocco and elsewhere and is as involved in Western politics as any NATO country. It is therefore logical to assume that soon a new Spain will emerge, revealing a reoriented political policy and a new social and economic structure.' I visited the beautiful city of Santiago del Compostella. As far as the course went, I recorded in my diary: 'and so I go on into dull days, when the brain is perpetually forced to listen to unnecessary facts. Is the course really doing me any good? Is my cowardly fatalistic approach to life being justified by my present existence?' (I should point out this kind of solipsism was a feature throughout NS of the personal diary.) One test I enjoyed was giving a lecture on the state of contemporary English drama. (I also thought of myself as a possible playwright!). This impressed the officer in charge of our course, Lt Commander Risden. He also liked my journal. Not to be true of all its officer readers - I was mortified later by an officer telling me to stop trying to write like Gertrude Stein and James Joyce - flattering in a way as I'd read neither. But I was impossibly under the influence of D H Lawrence. Well I passed, well enough, 9th out of some 25, allowing my second choice of posting, to the Mediterranean. In retrospect I think this was a far better choice than the Pacific. I recorded: 'Indeed I have passed but what about it? I have no feeling of pride, none of that sense of self-complacency that Captain Roper (Captain of HMS Ocean?) expected of us. Why should I?' So I was to be sent to Malta to join HMS Leverton, a mine-sweeper, as a midshipman.

The Cyprus Emergency

I arrived in Malta 16 May 1956. There was an alarming 4 hours when I feared I was to be appointed to LCT[3] HMS Baston, a soul-destroying posting, but eventually joined HMS Leverton. There was a frantic handover. As I

[3] LCT = Landing Craft Tank

recorded: 'I took in as much as I could about Correspondence, Gunnery, the cable-deck etc. (all to be my responsibilities) but it was remarkably little. I was just too tired.' A none too promising start to my time on the mine-sweeper. But a really interesting assignment lay ahead.

Here I must briefly explain the background to the Cyprus Emergency. Britain had come under strong Egyptian pressure to give up its Canal Colony and had pulled out by 1956: it transferred the centre of its East Mediterranean HQ to Cyprus. Maybe with the loss of Empire in India this no longer has quite the same strategic importance but we still took it all very seriously. Ernest Bevin had prioritised protection of our bases. Unfortunately this coincided with Enosis, the Greek Cypriot movement for Union with Greece, led by Archbishop Makarios. But it was a situation further complicated by the presence of a minority Turkish Cypriot community, opening up the possible and well tested imperial tactic of divide and rule. Both mainland Greece and Turkey were drawn into this island dispute. All of this was familiar to NSUYs through our study of contemporary affairs. This is how I recorded it (I was still being encouraged to see things through official naval eyes): 'As I see it, it is a problem of mob nationalism finding expression in ENOSIS. Harding (the Governor of Cyprus) must preserve order and try to come to some agreement with Makarios. Britain cannot acknowledge Cypriot right to self-determination yet, because of prestige and because the Cypriots do not know how to govern themselves and would not do so in a way favourable to NATO'. By 23

November 1955 I recorded in the official journal; 'Archbishop Makarios has said, though not officially, that he is ready to assume talks with Harding. But it is just possible that he will find himself in a position similar to that of Martin Luther, who started a revolt the violence of which he never contemplated. As a result he came down heavily on the side of authority, condemning the rioting peasantry. I only hope the Archbishop does the same.' (I had been an early modernist in my studies at 'A' level.) Lt Commander MacDonald (Leeds Castle) commented tartly on this journal entry, 'you quote Makarios rather a lot - what about our government's view on the situation?' In fact, a guerrilla movement, EOKA, under General Grivas, joined the fray.

Our assignment in Cyprus was to patrol the coastline of Cyprus to stop the smuggling of arms into the island. Eden had in fact deported Makarios to the Seychelles before my arrival, an act which no doubt emboldened a belief he could deal with Nasser in an equally high-handed way. In my time in Cyprus I came to revise my understanding of the problem. Here was a typical late imperial struggle, though nowhere so serious as in Malaya or Kenya.

So to the first of several journeys from Malta to the Eastern Mediterranean. To quote from my personal diary: 'I stood a little dazed as we left harbour acting as a modern figurehead. I left practically everything to my buffer who thank God is a most efficient chap.' I automatically became Officer of the Watch. To quote: 'The desolate coast-line of Crete was less of interest for its rugged repellent beauty than for its adequacy in providing fixes.' No time for writing poetry, though at night-time I reflected, 'all was intangibly calm at night. In the pattern of the stars I felt security, with a recognition of humanity stirring the ceaseless wrong ambitions of our souls.' So to Cyprus. To quote: 'The coastline as we came in from the south to Famagusta looked quite deserted. Was this really the island torn with fear and suspicion, with unnatural hatred because of the irrationality and bungling of a few men?'

I'll be very selective of the Cyprus experience. It was to be in two stages, the minesweeper patrol, and then, following my contraction of dysentery through foolishly swimming in Beirut harbour and hospitalisation at the RAF hospital Akrotiri, a shore based assignment in Nicosia.

Getting to know Famagusta was just a little alarming. First the Turkish quarter, to quote, 'feeling a little odd with a loaded pistol around my waist it was all just a little bit ragged. I wanted to see the inside of the mosque but felt that to enter armed would be a great mark of disrespect'. So further into the city: 'I don't mind admitting I felt distinctly nervous. I had horrible visions of soft-footed Cypriots encircling me in the silence, a silence I would not have the courage to shatter with my loaded pistol. However the Army were so inefficient in providing transport that by the time it arrived my irritation had dispelled my fear.' However, I was sympathetic to the Army: to quote: 'the Army has got far the worst of this Cyprus deal. They are lucky if they get any leave at all and the full force of Cypriot hatred falls on them. They live in a world of light, dry, khaki colours, monotonous and soul-destroying. Yet they seemed to go about their jobs comparatively cheerfully. There are about 150,000 of them here which is an unnatural amount. All because of a few hundred men. The world is indeed peculiar.'

And not once did we intercept any arms. I wrote one of my better poems about our boarding party intercepting a Syrian fishing boat.

There was a revealing racial incident whilst visiting an army camp. Many sailors got drunk and one of our crew was accused of throwing a knife at a Turk. To quote: 'Frankly at the time I thought this to be untrue although later it was confirmed. The whole village clustered around and I had visions of a full-scale fight. Very kindly they brought out chairs, placing them in a significant semi-circle as if we were about to take our places at a trial.' Then one of our crew firmly grasped the Turk in question, 'drivelling', to quote, 'that he had taken him under arrest for accusing a sailor without being able to substantiate his case. It was a brilliantly dramatic move. Eventually the incredible situation dissolved into the sea and the sailors returned - Bradbury, the only non-swimmer present, nearly drowning himself in the process. Fortunately there was an army chap standing by who had won the BEM for a sea rescue.'

The only pleasing part of the unfortunate though amusing affair was the revelation of strange loyalties in the men. 'The Stokers said it was always they that got it in the neck. All were indignant that they should be accused of drawing a knife on "a dirty Cyp". Above all they were for standing up for themselves as sailors. A few rude words were passed about the tolerance of the British approach. Indeed the officers were in disgrace for not assuming a stronger position in the affair. Somehow they all got back, somehow we got to sea that night.'

Once cured of dysentery - it was a rare strain and took weeks to clear up - I was posted to Maritime HQ, Nicosia, 'the throbbing heart, the quick-thinking brain, the nervous network of naval activities in Cyprus', as I ironically described it.

Here is my account of the journey from Akrotiri. 'The silence of the bus was strangely tense. And when someone whistled there was something almost profane in the noise. I sat right forward determined to take immediate charge in any emergency. With interest I scanned the roadsides lit by the small searchlight of the escort and our own headlights. In some places the bark of the tree was bitten into by barbed wire. I don't think I was afraid but I was a little bit annoyed when we lost our escort and every overhanging rock was a possible ambush. Eventually I reached the hotel Majestic.'

There were a few political conversations with Cypriots. One with a Turkish Cypriot, a man, in his 40s, married with five children, ex-Army, had fought against the Germans and was a POW for 3 years. To quote: 'I casually asked him what he thought of the Cyprus affair. His philosophy was plain. For every Turk they kill we kill five. Do you see? His eyes burned with feeling. I tried very hard to make him see the futility and short-sightedness of this policy. He convinced me, however, of the importance of the Turks in the island. All our families, he proceeded, now have five children or more, and in ten years time we will form half the population'. In hindsight, rather optimistically, I suggested a new friendship between the communities had to be fashioned, recognising that the Turks cannot leave the island.

Then a conversation with a Greek Cypriot. To quote: 'A most intelligent and strangely sensitive person. A man of the world much hardened by extensive travelling in West Africa. I tried to persuade him out of his ENOSIS position. He said Cyprus wanted to be boss in her own home. I argued, why does she want to throw the British out and subdue herself to badly organised poverty-ridden Greece? Our historical and cultural relationships. I can only enquire if this is a feeling common to all Greek Cypriots and if so, are they feelings which assume a greater importance than economic needs? He said they did. An interesting fact I was unaware of, Greece had refused Cyprus in 1918. I tried to prove to him that Greece had no fundamental interest in Cyprus. Her spirit was at the moment one of exclusive nationalism. Once Cyprus was in the hands of Greece it would fall into economic decay. The fact of having MPs at Athens would have no effect on her economic well-being. Surely it would be better for Cyprus to bide her time and actually acquire a realistic self-government maintaining fruitful ties with the Commonwealth? He was justifiably cynical about this. He said British newspapers and colonial administrators kept saying there is no Cyprus problem simply because there was no violence. It was because of this crass blindness that Cypriot frustration broke away from passive conferences into a policy of violence.' Maybe I was more conditioned than I knew by the official line!

I overheard a terrorist incident. To quote: 'bomb explodes. At first I ignore it, continue reading in my room. Then I realise and the appalling closeness of death fills the air. I listen to the barking dogs, the slightly raised voices of those accustomed to such sounds. I get up and ask an Englishman, "was that a bomb"? Indifferently he says, "there were two of them." The American still lies in his bed, unconcerned, uninterested. I return to my room and write these words. Can I relax? At first the noise of the fire engine, the sudden accumulation of army cars disquietens me. The wind fills the humid air in protest. My sweat-ridden body is grateful. I return to my book. An English family returns to the hotel. "Did you hear the bomb?" they say. I lean out of the window to listen to words spoken prosaically: "I'm safe, so what does it matter?"'

I visited another army camp and here I will conclude on Cyprus. To quote: 'Superficially it did not look too bad. At least tents are cooler than a minesweeper's cabin. We may be at the mercy of the inconstant sea but they are subjected to inconveniences through sun and rain. The rain dissolves the camp into mud. They walk through mud, they sleep in mud. Can one wonder if they are a little rough in handling suspects? But a vicious circle is inevitably created, hate breeding hate, until there will be no future generation who can forget our tyranny and we will leave the island for ever stained with dishonour.'

I fear I took my eye off the Cyprus story and have no solution to offer to a conflict still unresolved. In 1960

Cyprus became independent, Britain retaining its strategic bases - still in use in the Libyan imbroglio - but with no resolution of the communal problem. It has been compared to Northern Ireland, with the Greeks as the Protestant ascendancy and the Turks as the Catholics. Things came to a crisis with Grivas resurrecting Enosis and engineering the downfall of Makarios and so to his second deportation. This prompted in 1974 the Turkish invasion, with Cypriot troops no match for its army and so to the partition between north and south, the UN acting as mediators in the Green zone. One good thing to come out of this was the fall of the junta in Greece and the restoration of civilian rule.

In time I was appointed to HMS Forth, a submarine depot ship moored at Msida creek in Malta. This was out of the proverbial frying pan into the fire, for ahead lay Suez.

Suez

If my personal experience of Suez will not alter any of its grand narratives it does add some telling details. Of course it does not follow from being present at a world event like Suez that one is better informed as to what was going on. At no stage was I aware, for example, of the secret deals at that villa in the Paris suburb of Sèvres, 22 October 1956, between Britain, France and Israel. In retrospect I doubt if I had much insight into French motivation of socialist Prime-Minster Guy Mollet's Jewish and Israeli sympathies, of Foreign Minister Pineau's mistaken belief that removing Nasser would help end the war in Algeria against the FLN. I think all along we assumed we were there to reopen the canal and place it under some international control. I had little grasp though of how Britain and France came to act alone, how relationships with NATO and America had broken down - Eden indeed would have been hard pressed to say whom he hated the more, Nasser or Dulles-and with the UN. Admittedly we welcomed UN intervention and delusionally supposed our invasion force might become part of UNEF, the UN police force, but Indian hostility, Krishna Menon to the fore, put paid to that. But we doubted if the UN force would be ready soon enough, and by then it was too late anyway to stop our invasion.

But equally I suspect I was unaware of why Eden's administration attached so much importance to the Canal, with 70% of its shipping being British, and it being seen as the lifeline for oil. With Nasser being cast in the role of a 1930s dictator, Eden saw Britain, besides questions of prestige, battling for its very survival. Of course much of this was a misreading: Egypt was perfectly capable of running the Canal and with one exception, Israel, respected its status as an international waterway.

Friends always tease me that in time I shall be hauled before the International Court at The Hague for war crimes. Here is my apologia.

Did we in fact have much advance knowledge? Here is an entry in my private diary for 1 August. I was still in Cyprus. To quote: 'What is happening? Are we moving rapidly towards a foolish war? I was suddenly afraid when I heard HMS Eagle had come out to Cyprus. Other forces are standing by. Does Nasser still laugh in glee at his masterstroke in nationalising the canal? We deserved this rebuff. Our foolish policy over the Aswan dam showed us for what we were, political propagandists, forced into acts of superficial philanthropy through fear. But please God spare us war. Let not petty disturbances, border incidents, set flame to smouldering jealousies, irrational discontents. Let us not slide into war.' (Again I doubt if I appreciated that Nasser saw the Aswan dam as his main priority and though nationalising the Canal Company was indeed a nationalist gesture, the main reason for doing so was to raise funds for the dam once the World Bank had turned down its initial offer of a loan.)

'What makes it so horribly and frighteningly near is not the attitude of people: it is the steady accumulation of warlike facts that stare at me in the newspapers, shout at me from wirelesses, creep so casually into conversation.'

13 September

'Oh how I tried to see the way out of this Suez crisis. But I meet overpowering barriers of crying emotional demands. Please God give this sinful world a peace it hardly deserves.'

20 September

A reference to the so called Suez Canal User's Association. To quote: 'For the success of this insane idea a large ship is required as an accommodation for the pilots and as an HQ for its organisation. HMS Forth, in all her glory, was chosen. Complete panic. For two days extra supplies were being taken on board. Boats here and there but rarely where they were wanted. Officers screeching at one another, or else leaving the ship with little reluctance. It looks as if we are to stay in Msida creek after all.'

And indeed, Forth at this point goes on a trip to Sicily - no doubt, I now realise, to prove its sea-worthiness - and Suez is not mentioned again till November.

And now I take up a narrative of my role in Operation Musketeer, a massive amphibious exercise, modelled on the D-day landings, one entailing 100,000 men, 130 warships, including 6 aircraft carriers, more than a 100 freighters carrying nearly 20,000 vehicles and a multitude of landing crafts. There was seen to be a real risk of escalation into World War 111, and this would be a nuclear war.

I did think of resigning my commission but in the end my curiosity as a historian, to be a witness to history in the making, got the better of my moral conscience.

1 November

To quote: 'Now we are sailing into a war, a war I do not believe in but as yet insufficiently disbelieve in to try and leave the Navy. The Eastern Mediterranean seems very far away and so does the bloodshed and pointless death.

We assumed we were heading for Cyprus so when the Captain, Commander Stopford, announced over the tannoy on leaving Valetta harbour that we were in fact in a state of war and heading for Port Said, several Maltese stewards jumped overboard - this they had not bargained for.'

This was a 900 mile journey, 6 days for the slowest ships. There has been much last minute juggling of dates of departure. We had to get there by the 6th to coincide with the military invasion.

2 November

To quote: 'But even if I don't believe in this war I am strangely excited by it all. Possibly for commonplace reasons, the atmosphere, the study of men in danger, the danger to life.'

'I was asleep when we weighed anchor and proceeded to the Levant. I suppose the normality of everything reflects on the correctness of the machine-like nature of naval society. Only an unnatural community can readily adapt to the conditions of war.'

In fact, Forth was far from warlike. To quote: 'various people were asleep on watch and few ratings were available for departmental needs. Strange it was to walk into the stale atmosphere of below decks. Sailors had crashed into every conceivable place, on the side of ladders, in hammock stowages. This was a ship at war and refusing to realise the fact.'

'The Captain gave us to the best of his knowledge a summary of the operation and of Forth's task. At least we will not moor alongside Port Said until some success is shown in the psychological war. All I can say is that I am sufficiently psychologically upset by the information that Egypt has submarines. Until we join up with the convoy we are defenceless.'

Such defences as we owned were to prove woefully inept. Several times over, I record, the failing of the 4.5 pom poms. On one occasion the crew trained the wrong way. On another, such failings proved a blessing in disguise. We evidently lacked the expertise to differentiate between French Mystères and Egyptian Russian MIGs and when one such Mystère failed to identify itself we would have fired at it had the pom pom not gone over its firing arc. (Is it possible the plane was one *en route* to provide air cover for Israel as part of the secret deal, and hence it could not identify itself?)

3 November

To quote: 'Still war is remote but coming nearer. I was disturbed by the CPO who told me there was little chance of escape from my action station in the gunroom. Feet would push me down. How repulsive! But I slept through exercise gas gas gas for I was very tired after a dull middle watch. But even now I can spend part of the afternoon sunbathing on the quarterdeck. A sparrow hawk is using us as his transport but is still timid. How will it react to gunfire?'

4 November

To quote: 'Am writing this as we closed up at dusk action stations. No-one ever comes to visit the gunroom and indeed am of little use down here. But it does mean my sleep is not too readily broken. And one does need sleep, being closed in defence stations with one in three watch.'

'Still all is calm and once again No1 gun trained the wrong way. We are but 200 miles from Suez and no sign of enemy forces. Have we already broken their resistance? The decision of the UN to establish a large police force should be sufficient to deter any new outburst in the Middle East. (How did I know that?) The Arabs are stranded from the Russians by the tragic war in Hungary. I am afraid Hungary will once again retreat into the night of despair. Can we risk the destruction of the world for their sake? I am now all for peace and have not the self-sacrifice to support a policy of assistance for Hungary.'

5 November

To quote: 'Guy Fawkes day. We have just made contact by radar with the convoy. But no cause for consolation. The main convoy is centred on HMS Ranpura and HMS Forth, gash tankers, tugs, LSTs[4] - a most unwarlike force. Just have to cross our fingers no Egyptian plane comes near and pray for carrier force coverage.

It was a lovely sky, a shining freshening blue with freely swept white tresses of cloud. Why I cannot imagine, but I was reminded of Alice in Wonderland.'

6 November

To quote: 'Ships all around us. At its very last stage this apparent pleasure cruise to Port Said ceased to be.' I refer to the growing complexity of the news and the possibility of Russian intervention. Might it yet, I ask, turn into a struggle of Goliath (us) and David (Egypt)? To quote: 'How idiotically in the wrong we are. Why can we not walk hand in hand with the UN and drop this arrogant

---

[4] LST = Landing Ship Tank

independent approach? I pray to God to give wisdom to our leaders.'

I refer to 'the action of the RAF and Army who are now putting out the Raleigh cloak for our entrance. Smoke, gunfire, told us of action. But we could hardly see Egypt yet.'

'Now we are waiting to enter Port Said, a sitting duck of a convoy, surely the most extraordinary war of all time. A superb chance for Russia to cripple what strength France and Britain have left.'

(Obviously in hindsight I was unaware of the destruction of the Egyptian airforce on the ground and the extent to which Russia was stymied by Hungary. And Russia did not in fact have the range of a missile strike. Still, there was a real risk of Russian intervention.)

'Maybe all is now over. Goliath is afraid and has given the order for a ceasefire. Nevertheless we are staying here until the UN comes in.' Eden had bowed to all kinds of pressure and had accepted a cease-fire by midnight on the 6th. France, very reluctantly, had to follow suit. (We were in a way hoist with our own petard, the given reason for intervening, part of that secret Sèvres deal, had been to separate the armies of Israel and Egypt, and this had lost its rationale: Israel had obtained its own objectives and Egypt had withdrawn its army from Sinai. But, of course, it was the threatened economic collapse with the run on the pound that forced our acceptance of a cease-fire.)

7 November

Nearly a disaster on entering Port Said. We were facing the wrong way and had the option of turning the long way round or a very tight inward turn towards HMS Ranpura. Almost fatally we chose the latter. To quote: 'we almost rammed Ranpura on trying to enter harbour. Of course I was amused that the Captain wrapped himself around the stanchion post like a wet rag and the Navigating Officer quivered like burnt paper in a draft.' (Not my best prose.) This could have been a very newsworthy start to our Port Said mission.

To quote again: 'But everything seems so utterly worthless now. For I see we were wrong ever to invade this land, we the support group to an aggression.'

'Well, we made it into harbour only to find it in a real mess, with numerous ships sunk, 47 in fact, and two bridges destroyed, blocking access to both ends of the canal. This was Nasser's response to the threat of invasion, and of course made nonsense of our attempt to keep the canal functioning.'

I was to stay to the very end of this operation, December 22, when we formally handed Port Said to the UNEF. All military personnel left, even the crews of the salvage ships.

Let me summarily describe my Suez experience. In terms of the action itself.

'I visited the war zone, the destruction of the Arab shanty town very obvious.' To quote: 'the charnel remnant of large areas became tragic when in the rubble you saw helpless old women searching for their possessions, children playing on a seesaw, ignorant of it all.' I'll limit description of the cemetery: 'these dead were for me still grotesquely alive.'

I very much took to Port Fouad which the French had occupied. It had been the former French quarter. I tried to catch the eye of the ferryman: to quote: 'to steal any glance of hatred, any glance of friendliness, but all I met was remoteness, not even curiosity. We were nothing extraordinary. There was inertia, an indifference pervading the town.'

We visited the HQ of the French. I'm not quite sure of the geography of this but then we went up to the front line, I realise now on the western side. The ceasefire came when we were but 20 miles down the 100 mile long canal, certainly not as far as Ismailia, let alone Suez. En route we met a very tough French parachute regiment. Now quoting: 'So down the canal road. Taking in a new scene. Not one of variety. Always with the canal itself, strangely thin, the Treaty Road, the murky sweet water canal taking water to Port Said, the morbid salt marsh lands and the desert stretching way to the Gaza strip and Israel. All along the canal were stationed small groups of French and English soldiers, fishing, bathing, just dreaming. Eventually we came right to the front line, a misleading name, however. In all there were 60 people at the front, the Egyptians but 600 yards away, stationed behind a large wedge of land. I felt sorry for the men here but they were confident and casual about it all, convinced of the basic cowardice of the Egyptians. Extraordinary - I go right to the front line of the Anglo-Egyptian war and there meet an old Greshamian, Ian Loggie.'

A later visit to the town, December 1. To quote: 'Opening up. Many more street vendors and shops open. But walking through the back streets I grew conscious of a new approach towards us by the Egyptians. Previously they were indifferent. Now they stared unsmilingly but unmaliciously. But I did notice a gently mocking light, saying, "we now know where you stand".' Here I also encountered three trucks of UN troops, to quote, 'fresh-faced Scandinavians, radiant in their light blue helmets'.

On another occasion we visited the dockyard warehouses. Later, after I'd joined the LST HMS Striker, I was to learn from RM Commando NCO's, how rapaciously they'd been looted - Customs Officers had turned a blind eye as they returned with handfuls of diamonds. All I looted was a paperweight in the shape of a sphinx and a battered Everyman edition of David Hume's *On Human Understanding*.

HMS Forth was HQ ship also of the press. At an early stage my diary records my arranging a BBC interview with a naval officer. I came to learn how news stories are made - blown up out of very thin material. James Morris was the Guardian journalist.

Did I have a role at Suez? Well, twice I put my life on the line - on Day 1 of our arrival being dispatched at night to trace and kill a suspect frogman trying to blow up a salvage ship Le Photen. Later I learnt its sentry had nearly taken a pot shot at me. At the very end of the mission, dispatched to remove an Egyptian flag from the statue of De Lesseps, having to run the gauntlet of sporadic Egyptian gunfire. I and another midshipman in fact failed to do so and later the statue was blown off its pedestal.

If I have any claims to making any contribution at Suez it was through my appointment as Fleet Mail boat officer, taking the mail to that strange assemblage of salvage ships that had materialised. Sadly, no-one told me that engine oil needed to be topped up, and regrettably the engines of two Egyptian pilot boats seized up. A war crime indeed.

And so we returned to Malta, the last ship of the original task force to leave, not quite in time for Christmas. Nothing in my remaining seven months was to match for drama Cyprus and Suez.

This is Hugh Thomas's judgement on Suez: 'the spectacle of over one hundred thousand men setting off for a war which lasted barely a day has few parallels in the long gallery of military imbecility.' It was 'doomed from the start'. (*The Suez Affair* 1971 pp183-4)

Was National Service worth it?

To return to that unanswered question. I think the most obvious point to make about NS was its taking place during adolescence, the most impressionable years. Inevitably it made a huge impact, be it positive or negative. I have made no reference so far to social life. Whilst on the lower deck the height of one's ambition was a meal in the NAAFI. As an officer there were numerous bibulous nights in ward-room and gun-room. As shore based officers in Malta we were in great social demand and I went to more gigs than at any other stage of life, rock and rolling the night away. I acquired a passion for travel. Apart from Malta and Cyprus, both beautiful islands, the Navy took me to Lebanon, Syria, a great deal of Italy - visits to the South almost turned me into a Risorgimento historian - Naples, Rome, Venice and the Tyrol - a lovely combination - and I travelled over-land home after leaving, through Italy, via Orvieto, Assisi, Florence, and Southern Germany, the Romantic way, Rothenberg to Wurzburg, so to Augsburg. But the main claim made for NS is its role in its maturing us, but this I dispute. In many ways this was an experience I felt a need to unscramble. Maybe I hit NS at a very negative moment. I encountered in the Navy a still ossified hierarchical social system - and the diary reveals I was genuinely shocked by this - but of course the Armed forces were to become both more professional and more meritocratic. I was exposed to a Cold War ideology at its most rigid, and to a degree I guess I accepted the need to subvert a totalitarian system, but then ahead lay détente. I did resent being caught up in the last spasms of Empire, but of course post-Suez it all began to unravel, with Macmillan's wind of change speech and the transformation of Empire into Commonwealth.

Trevor Royle concludes of these two years: 'it was a time when National Servicemen were supposed to be enjoying the best years of their lives.' For me National Service was the most different experience of my life and for that, despite the caveats, I do indeed look back on it as a valuable time.

Antony – Upper Yardsman (1955)

7
LATE ADOLESCENCE

If this is a period of rebelliousness it is even more a time of confusion. If belatedly a rebel at school, I was shortly to face the even more punitive and hierarchical Royal Navy. In fact I had a strong streak of conformity, otherwise why would I have settled for being a midshipman? In abstract terms I was caught in the classic struggle between Freedom and Authority. The rebellion turned inwards and a conventional adolescent crisis of identity. In broad brush terms, was I to look outwards and seek some engagement with the world or turn inwards and be detached? It was an ancient battle between social commitment and alienation. The wish to be a poet was strong, if divided between writing verse drama or poetry. Looking back at personal diaries which begin and are written sporadically afterwards from 14 September 1955, I am clearly caught up with contemporary affairs, embattled over the role of the arts and increasingly conflicted over religion. Here I am running parallel with my National Service up until going to Oxford. It is by way of an intellectual Odyssey. It is of course embarrassing with taking myself far too seriously.

Ineluctably we were all being drawn into the Cold War. I wrote a long dialogue between a Christian of uncertain faith and a Communist. It was no doubt prompted by a home visit from Hugh Maddox. We debated the ways forward for world peace, the role of love or charity, the role of socialism. The problem lay in man's selfishness, and the way in which a socialist state would pander to materialism and the inherent risk that bureaucracy will stifle any feelings of self-sacrifice. The answer lay in men of integrity practising a gospel of love: 'it really does seem as if Eliot's concept of an aristocracy of the Godly is the first stage in the route to world peace.' The danger lay in an even greater suffering in the Soviet satellite states, a risk of their losing any independence of mind: 'these people will be so utterly indoctrinated as to be unapproachable, impervious to our western ideals.' If this suggested western indoctrination, I go on: 'we must not approach this in a missionary spirit but with a spirit of real love. They themselves must finally decide whether we are right or wrong, although we know we are right and we believe they will perceive this rectitude.' Faint echoes here of J S Mill!

So to my dialogue between a Christian and Karl a Communist, a reflection on my own divided self, on the future of international Communism. Karl gives the lie to the accusation that Communism works through hate (did I mean class hatred?) but rather through its ability to meet material needs. And Karl's response to the charge that this will still antagonise: 'Communism does not excite itself over time. We can wait. We fight for the happiness of future generations. Time is on our side.' 'We spread the doctrine and obtain followers in all areas of poverty and unrest abroad and at home we educate the young. You see, we can wait.' He continues: 'You may say that the fear of communism is on your side but that is where you are wrong. Fear merely breeds unrest and that is where communism thrives.' Karl also points to the loss of independent thought in the west, with the wireless, TV, film, leading to intellectual sterility. (Had I got hold here of the ideas of Marshall McCluhan?) The TUC is seen as strengthening the power of communism. The Christian is here seen on the back foot (quite why is unclear) and foresees a world of 1984, 'vast conflicts between the continents for ever and entrenched dictatorships.' Karl is unimpressed: 'I must remind you the Communists are not disturbed by time. Marxism is the creed of economic necessity. Eventually one man will be the sole ruler of the world. Marxism is the idealism of materialism. That one man will be the God of men.' The Christian is appalled: 'the final result will be the creation of one dead soul', a Man-God: 'the final communist state will be the complete slavery of the mind.' The alternative is Christianity. Karl sees this as preposterous: 'you do not seriously think that a creed that preaches self-abnegation, indeed poverty, is going to unite a materialistic world'. The Christian responds: 'in a Christian world man retains his individuality, both in his relationship to fellow men and to his God: the perpetual conflict between good and evil must last to the Final Coming. Here lies the freedom of the mind and the senses'. But he concedes time is not on his side and that we have to respond to suffering: 'but whereas you can only turn to the dried up leaves of the Manifesto, I can turn to my Father in Heaven.' Karl is not phased: 'eventually we will even be able to dispense with the God-man. Men will be so aware of the economic advantages of communism that he will educate his children in its charm, the creed will be forever perpetuated, man will grow to love man, his natural distrust and selfishness forever banished.' 'Where is the programme, the technique, the leader in Christianity to compare with their parallel in Communism?'

Well, I rather think Karl won this debate and I detect some anticipation of the approach of Theodor Adorno. In his *Aesthetics* he foresaw the resolution of class conflict in an idealised democratic classless society. Nevertheless, as 1989 was to show, time was not in fact on the side of the Communist world.

The influence of acting in those school plays was greater than I knew. Writing a play became one obsessive form of self-expression. During my NSUY training I chose to give my talk on the theatre today. My theme was of the greatness of a play lying in its illusion of reality. What do we expect from going to the theatre? Do we want some sense of the play as a reflection of our reality, though without it being didactic, or merely an awareness of the beautiful and a form of escapism? I cited Graham Greene's *The Living Room* as an example of the former, the plays of Anouilh and Christopher Fry the latter. But the dramatists who underlay the best of contemporary theatre were Chekhov and Ibsen. Shaw got it right when he asserted: 'the illusion of reality - that is what matters.' But Shaw could never get beyond the didactic and write tragedy: his *St Joan* fails through the didacticism of the last act. Shaw never allowed feeling to prevail over reason. And if a play were to reflect too narrowly 'modernity', as in those 1930s plays by Auden and Isherwood, they likewise fail. They have in the way of Shakespeare to be rooted in popular culture. In Shakespeare the poetry transcends our lives.

Not that modern theatre should imitate Shakespeare, for imitation leads to decadence. Only the Greek tragediennes are his rival. I ended with Eliot. I found *Murder in the Cathedral* too much of an interior conflict, hence not real. *The Family Reunion* tried to embrace the tones of modern speech. *The Cocktail Party* explores various forms of self-deception. Was I in fact endorsing Eliot as dramatist? I ended, possibly to ingratiate myself with my Naval Officer assessor, with a side swipe at the new theatre of the angry young men: 'the purely condemning, angry destructive play is undesirable.' Did my own attempt at a play live up to these standards?

I'd attempted a verse drama, unfinished and unentitled at the time of my call-up. It's a story of political ambition and the corruption of power. Quite clearly *Macbeth* lies behind it. It has the feel of a 20th century *coup d'état*, but then I had not studied the 20th century, the characters bear no relationship to the Nazi gutter elite, though do have some kinship with the Prussian aristocracy of the German resistance and the personnel of the July 1944 bomb plot. But I suspect the real inspiration was the enigmatic figure of Count Wallenstein in the Thirty Years War.

It is prefaced by a pastoral scene, one Richard and Carol canoodling, only to be interrupted by Father Joseph. A political debate ensues, Joseph commenting on the way present day material prosperity reflects well on the current government. *Richard* responds in proto-fascist style:

But I grow tired of this peaceful way of life
I feel my heart rebel against this placidity
I dream of greater things
I am proud of my native land
But in our love of peace
We have ceased to be a power in the world
Sometimes I dream of days when our armies
Try to bind the nations in our flag
And in their hour of victory
I stride with them across the plains of Europe
To regain our country's pride

Joseph rebukes him

Foolish boy, drive such thoughts from your mind
Or else they will be driven from your skull
By shrapnel or by bullets for such ideas
Will always lead to war
Oh Richard I remember days
When our lovely landscape was laid bare with wounds
Which the green grass only heals in times of peace
When armies swarmed like killer ants across our fields
Leaving behind a waste as barren as a rockless shore
Surely you must realise what we owe to our peace
We owe our prosperity and our happiness

Then *Richard* introduces the theme of the play, rumours of a power struggle at court over the succession.

I believe a new and warlike blood
Will enter soon the heart of our country
And its pulse will rouse our land from apathy

Joseph disputes this

Count Fredrick will follow Leopold
And he is a lover of peace

Now the scene shifts to Prince Leopold's palace. On its terrace is Karl, a rugged man of 35 and Heinrich, Duke of Roxenberg, an exceptionally handsome man of the same age
They reflect on the succession

Karl

And so Heinrich Prince Leopold is at last dying
After thirty years of good and peaceful government
Thirty years of peace
Thirty years of apathy

Heinrich

Quiet, Karl, the tone of your voice
Disturbs the shadows of dark death
That makes grey the evening sky
This night has come to bear his soul away

Karl observes, this is the moment they have been waiting for, with Heinrich to be appointed successor, the promised leader that the youth of the nation desires

But *Heinrich* interjects

What about Count Frederick?
No, Karl, Death is not the time for ambition
It is a time of resignation, possibly despair
Yes we entertain these hopes
But we must bide our time

Karl insists the moment to seize power has come, his personal army is at his disposal, Prince Leopold by his indifference to war has made it easy for a lover of war to assume power.
They are interrupted by *Maurice*, one of Leopold's courtiers. In his view, we must reconcile ourselves to the inevitable, and that Leopold's calm acceptance of death, far from being sad, is inspiring

Heinrich asks why Count Frederick is absent.

Maurice replies

Leopold seems determined to avoid his name
As if he knew some loathsome secret of him
And indeed rumour has thrown some cruel cloud over his name, that he is implicated in a plot,
to seize power by a military *coup d'état*

Karl declares this will make Heinrich the successor, Heinrich is disbelieving, but Maurice sees only Heinrich as continuing Leopold's policy of peace

They retire to the inner court leaving Karl on the terrace

Heinrich

It is not yet but it must be I
For who else?
Rupert is young and inexperienced
O God I feel like Macbeth, a mere pawn
Swallowed up in some awful repetition of time
But if there is a Banquo, surely he is Count Frederick
But he is no more a rival. Who is Macduff? Prince Rupert?
Who is Lady Macbeth? O she is Karl

Heinrich shows remorse at deceiving Leopold that he shares his policy of peace.

But I do not face my life to come
As bravely as you face your death
Fate, bide my ruin for a while

A servant enters the room to prepare it for Leopold's death

Karl re-enters announcing Leopold has but hours to live

It is vital Heinrich that you do no foolish thing
For the jealous eyes of the court will be on you
Deceive Prince Rupert for he knows you are my friend
And I am his enemy
It would be easy
For Prince Leopold to change his mind

The court enters. Prince Rupert, a young man of 25, of an emotional and romantic temperament. Count Fredrick's absence is noticed and Karl provides the explanation.

Prince Rupert

Count Frederick has retired to his country estate
As if in disgrace, though he denies his guilt
Leopold will not however charge him with high treason
It is hard to believe
These accusations of Count Karl and even if they are not false
I am certain Count Frederick is a reluctant figurehead
Rather than the cause.
Better to win him back as a supporter of the new government

Prince Leopold reflects on his life's work

I wish to die
Knowing my country will continue to live in peace
For that has been the pre-eminent aim of my life
The task has been hard, perpetual frustration of ambition
Pacifism stirring angry nationalism
But you know the tale

He names his successor, Heinrich, Duke of Roxenberg. Karl agrees, Rupert supports.

Leopold and Heinrich are left alone.

Leopold

How still the night is, Heinrich, like a huge sea
Becalmed by summer. How quiet our city is.
Heinrich I shall die an old and contented man

But *Heinrich* cannot let Leopold die with false hopes

For ten years of torture I have deceived you
Into believing that I admire your policy of peace
For ten years I have stood by your side in Council
Or alone in our conversations and always
I have deceived you and repressed myself
Ten years of agony that forbids me now
To send you to your death deluded
I am proud, Leopold, and the proud are always weak
Your age has denied me glory
O you are right Leopold, it is easy, terrifyingly easy
To fail in a conflict with ambition

Leopold

What madman have I sent to govern you my people?

Heinrich

No I am not mad, Leopold but determined
To fulfil a ghastly desire. I have no choice.
Ambition has conquered my heart and guides my life
I will make war on the world and I shall see
My name stamped in the dirt

Heinrich smothers Leopold with a cushion

The Court re-enters. Rupert comments on the look of peace on Leopold's face

Heinrich

He showed sudden reluctance at the final parting
The shades of death enclosed his soul
More quickly than he was prepared.
He died wishing to see sunrise on his native land.
He died Rupert wishing you were at his side

Prince Rupert acknowledges the pain in Heinrich's face

It is my will and duty always to be your servant
May sleep give rest and relief to your mind

Another soliloquy from *Heinrich*

Sleep and relief?
O no they are as distant as the sea's murmur
My dreams for life deprive me of their calm
O God, time has traversed the universe these last few hours

He recognises he has rejected God and commits himself to violence

O come Heinrich, we'll go laugh out the night
Planning hell-fire for foolish slobbering man

And that is as far as I got.

Act 11 would be about Karl and the corrupting exercise of power, Count Fredrick leading the opposition

Act 111 would be Heinrich's downfall and suicide.

Had I such ambitious men as Charles X11, Napoleon, Hitler in mind? Was this a kind of Pilgrim's Progress, with its characters as personified abstractions?

If the play was to work as tragedy we would have to feel sympathy for Heinrich and his self-destructive make-up.

Writing poetry took me beyond the concerns of the Cold War and power politics into a higher metaphysical quest, a search for values, for meaning. Admittedly much of the poetry was a vehicle for maudlin self-reflection and deeply embarrassing. Again, unfortunately, no doubt conditioned by reading Aldous Huxley and Evelyn Waugh, this was tied into questions of authenticity, and there is a constant moan at the lack of seriousness amongst my contemporaries. I wonder why so called sincerity was such an imperative. And, as I reassess the poetry, it is clear that anything of merit looked outwards and responded to real events rather than inwards and wallowing in self-pity. At the metaphysical level, the battle lay between the this-worldliness of a Stephen Spender and the other-worldliness of T S Eliot. At heart this was a religious debate.

I'd used the prize money from the Fordham Serious Verse prize to buy the Collected works of both Spender and Eliot. Spender's autobiography *World within World* both turned me towards the left and began to give shape to my as yet inchoate desire for a working class lover. (In fact Spender was bi-sexual and had a liking for glamorous boys, so this was a false message.) I later read his *The Destructive Element* and *The Making of a Poem*. I heard a brilliant British Council lecture by Nevil Coghill on Eliot. He spoke of Eliot's 'detached religion', (in fact Spender's phrase), and saw in Eliot the need for each generation to rebuild the church for itself, to rediscover the meaning of the Word. Eliot believed in the purification of the will. Did this mean to immure human will in the will of God? Coghill saw in the martyrdom of *Murder in the Cathedral* the way for man to escape his cyclical prison: 'the saint is the instrument of God and is entirely in his hands.' In *The Family Reunion* the Eumenides are not instruments of revenge but of God's love. Coghill felt *The Cocktail Party* had failed to bring out the happiness of marriage and a better ending would have been the birth of a child. I took to Coghill and saw him as a 'naturally unworldly man'. It's revealing how dominant those Eliot plays were. How was I reacting to these ideas?

Here is a diary entry for 22 January 1956:

'There is a vast mass of confused feeling which I cannot enter into, cannot consequently genuinely feel. Do I really believe in Christian regeneration? Do I really believe in world unity? Do I really believe in anything outside of my own self? How much do I feel?'

'Were I not to experience genuine empathy, I would sleight these feelings.'

I recorded a dream whilst still an Upper Yardsman. 'Am unable to face Eternity but God overcomes my fear. But who was that dark stranger striding through the pine trees, walking black through the sunless wood, the field of heaven was no more. I see a propaganda balloon trailing the message, The Kingdom of God cannot be until it is realised on earth. I turned to face the solitary messenger of the black pine trees. I dared not ask him who he was.'

The best of the poetry has this element of quest and here the deepest influence was D H Lawrence. I had been reading him early on in National Service. In a diary entry for 11 January 1957, responding to a reading of *The Plumed Serpent*, I write: 'I see him as my literary hero. I'm not so concerned with his philosophy of sex, important though it be. What satisfies me is his feeling, his acute awareness of other people, his identification with the environment, with the soul immersed in the world. It is the density, the darkness, the humidity, the oiliness of Mexico.' He had a disastrous influence on my writing style. Yet I failed to live up to Lawrence's sincerity: 'Lawrence's feelings make my present behaviour regrettable.' Housman was another who never compromised with a shallow society. 'Heine apparently did and so do I. This persistent search for authenticity.' (6 February 1957.) Was I turning into one of Osborne's angry young men? Because I was living by the values of others? 'You have to live by the values you have formed for yourself.' But I recognised 'the values I have created, values concerning a sincere interest in intellectual ideas, the development of social concerns, sincere feelings,these values are incompatible with the naval and social cliques.' If I were to give up this quest for sincerity, 'I will find life meaningless, I will be apathetic, I will grow untidy in all conceivable ways.' And I was clearly failing. 'Is all this Huxleyan? Am I a type of emotional snob, searching to create deep feelings for myself, but in point of fact incapable of undergoing anything profound?' The diary describes conversations with the talented pianist, Dorian Aroyo, Cambridge educated, challenging me with his considerable sophistication. But was I reaching out for values more substantial than this solipsism?

Post-Coghill, I saw the way out of my predicament as a return to Nature. It is necessary to appreciate the simplicity of things, flowers, birds, trees, the pastoral life. Somehow I must find that unity with purity. Re-reading *The Family Reunion* reactivated that missionary impulse but I doubted if it would last: 'eventually I should be compelled to leave the dark races and return to the land of the dead.' Then I seemed to pull all this together. I'd been to hear a performance of *Tosca*. I grasped what Spender meant by the Destructive element. 'It is Eliot's refusal to see a way of salvation through the contemporary world. Eliot's intuitions of the meaning of life can never be realised in a communication between men and their modern surroundings. It can only be by a direct relationship with the Reality, involving a divorce between man and the world around. What Spender looks for is the Creative element, one that links the Reality with this world. He also wants salvation through a modern medium.' My own conclusion was that the search of the Idealist for a dream world, tantalising but remote, is wrong-headed: we have to seek an ideal which can be realised in the world today. So has Spender's this-worldliness prevailed over Eliot's other-worldliness?

Alongside all this reflection on poetry and literary criticism lay a concern with religion. I'm rather surprised this took centre-stage. It is not as if religion had played much part in my upbringing. Both my parents were wholly indifferent to religion, though they did not stop my sister and me attending church. We used to wend our way past that pigsty and up a bridle path to St Lawrence's church in Elstree. Here was an impossibly flamboyant vicar who once took us off to one of those Earl's Court meetings of Billy Graham. I did not 'go forward' and indeed suspect the whole occasion left me with a lasting antipathy for expressions of evangelical faith. Of course both Kingshott and Gresham's had insisted on compulsory church and chapel attendance. I had been confirmed at Gresham's but was much more moved by my adult baptism. It was discovered I had no baptismal certificate. Father supposed, with the outbreak of the war, baptism had been overlooked. According to Catholic doctrine, I might have died and been sent to hell. Antony replaced Anthony. My former teacher at Kingshott, George Silver, who went on to be a priest and then a monk, tried to shape my Christian faith. The Navy did not insist on but did encourage church attendance. I can only see my obsessive worry over religion as an aspect of adolescence.

Was I still haunted by that vocational calling in CCF camp? There is a weird entry for 28th April 1957: 'it occurred to me at night walking to the Craigs that if I must have freedom, freedom from all religious conventions, all dogma, all ceremonies, and if I persist in a priestly missionary career, it is necessary to form a band of my own. And yet I must have patience. I must if needs be spend six years preparing for the active life of the vocation. I must tolerate the years of History, the matrix of all subjects. On this basis I must grow through theology, medicine, philosophy, philology. Not until the very end of my learning, not until I have studied comparative religion, dare I propound my own philosophy, dare I pose as the leader of a new religious sect.' Dear oh dear! Could I have really believed this? I should point out that at school no book had baffled me more than A C Bouquet's on comparative religion, and that explains why, indeed, in later life I did address this subject in some depth. Was all this in part anti-Catholic?

In Malta I was exposed to a very traditional Catholic faith. On Good Friday 1957 my friend Michael and I witnessed a religious procession: 'I was almost angry at seeing these over-dramatic floats of the Crucifixion, being flash-photographed by seedy Maltese, stared at by a pallid crowd. What should have been a reminder of a tragedy was almost a farce.' It evoked the Ku Klux Klan. I attended an open-air meeting led by the Archbishop of Malta in St Publius square, Floriana. It being May Day St Joseph, patron saint of workers, was on display. The words on the tannoy mingled with the cries of vendors: 'I felt I was walking through the conflicts of the world, of spirituality and materialism.' Beside the church an unattractive priest was haranguing the crowd. I realised later that here was the Church fighting back against the challenge of Mintoff's Labour party. On 5 May there was a celebration of St Publius himself, thousands of firework squids exploding inside the cathedral, warding off the devil. The Congregation were unfazed. How, I wondered, did Jesus himself remain calm in all this mayhem? All this was hardly likely to make Catholicism attractive. Still, my commentary is disagreeably xenophobic. Later my friend Patrick (Rashid) and I witnessed Pope Pius X11 being carried around St Peter's on his papal throne.

Was Anglicanism more attractive? I was clearly very excited by a sermon given by Revd Basil Watson in the Anglican cathedral on the afterlife. I came away absorbed by a sudden realisation of what the afterlife might be like. There was Eliot's warning: to seek for the wrong motive was to destroy the virtue of seeking. St Paul, authority on the Resurrection, claims the body loses its natural quality once it assumes its supernatural, a body as different from the natural as a blade of grass to a seed. Even so, we must appreciate the continuity of the body. We will still possess the power of self-expression. (I was suddenly terrified at the thought of the mental activity in the afterlife.) We must rid ourselves of any dream of Elysian Fields. The dying of our natural life gives birth to a new self, part of the love of God. Life in heaven will be a continual awareness of the love and glory of God. But this will involve the same necessity for continually dying. (Was this explained?) Will there be the same struggle? The greatest threat is self-annihilation, for surely Heaven must offer a release from that struggle. We all know the pleasure from some act of altruism. Is Heaven an eternity of that pleasure? It will indeed be wise to bend ourselves now towards Christianity for so incredible a reward. But back again to Eliot. There must be many who cut themselves off from eternity for the wrong expectations. Even so, the cynics are worse. How to convey the need for purposeful self-abnegation? Only years later did I read Theosophy's account of etheric, intermediate and subtle bodies.

In fact it was not theology but the fine arts that influenced the more my religious quest. It was at the home of my step-mother's relatives, the Craigs, through avid listening of the LP collection of Dr John Craig (a brilliant surgeon and tipped to be Malta's Governor), that I hugely extended my awareness of music. I'm astonished to discover that at this time Dorian Aroyo explained atonality to me: 'harmonic tension, not that of the usual chromatic climax, but of a continuous unrounded note, always leading somewhere, expectant, easily tormented.' Even so, I was unimpressed by Dorian's playing Bartok's chromatic developments: 'they seemed a little monotonous and required powerful intellectual concentration if interest was to be maintained.' I still struggled to grasp Bach as 'an angel of God', the words of a mysterious, unrecalled, Mr Nemi, who features quite often in the diary: 'I am far from even understanding the spiritual world embodied in Bach's music. How do we understand the Mystery? Beethoven provides a far greater sense of well-being because he linked humanity with spirituality. Bach but depicted the Mystery.' Yet even Beethoven was not wholly convincing: 'I really do not think Beethoven ever explained the Mystery to us. His is a tremendous expression of jubilation at witnessing the Heavens. And the greatest man of all will be he who creates the Heavens in his art. I think Michelangelo came closer than Beethoven.' I responded angrily to a question from another friend, Robert Tollemache, as to what is intellectual music: 'it means that the listener has an idea which is developed as a result of the potent argument of the music. It may be that an entirely abstract concept is held in play. It forces us to think. We are in danger of our emotions being overwhelmed. To relieve ourselves of the pain we must grasp the music with our intelligence. We must fight with Beethoven or be conquered.'

I was indeed overwhelmed by a piano recital by Shura Cherkassky, which seemingly reflected on Russia's tribulations. On my return to England I was to hear Dame Myra Hess play at the Proms Beethoven's Emperor Concert, 'bringing a difficult intellectual argument to a satisfactory conclusion.' Shostakovitch's 5th I saw as a 'tremendous struggle against despair. Man will only struggle into a paradise matted in blood and after much suffering.' But Shostakovitch was still compromising with the Soviet regime, 'the scherzo offering false optimism.' I had read a great deal on the lives of composers whilst recovering from dysentery in the RAF hospital in Cyprus at Akrotiri. Only in my retirement did I re-visit a wish to write about the lives of composers in the 20th century.

Did painting provide greater insight into the Mystery? Although there were no lectures on the history of art in school art classes, I'd come away with a love of Cezanne and Van Gogh, pictured in all those wonderful Phaidon books, and at some early stage, El Greco. One of my first foreign holidays took me to Bruges and a discovery of Flemish art. I was very fortunate in discovering the great art centres of Italy, Rome, Florence and Venice, long before the invasion of mass tourism. Venice became my favourite of the three after my first and best visit in a mist-laden January 1957, a visit that hugely enlarged my appreciation of European art. Another journey of discovery was my return to England following National Service through Naples, Rome, Orvieto, Assisi, Florence, and so through Northern Italy, into Southern Germany and home.

At this stage I was always drawn to earlier and Byzantine paintings and struggled with those of the Counter-Reformation and Baroque. In Venice, responding to the primitives: 'it's the simple mindedness that makes Christ twice size at the Last Supper which appeals to me. This is genuine popular art for the people.' Of Giovanni di Bologna: 'the hypnotic mystical gaze in the eyes of the saints. These are real eastern prophetic men. Love of colour for its own sake.' In those days you could just wander into the Basilica: 'it's Christ above the High Altar: the elemental religion of an age which saw the centrality of God. They saw God and not their feelings about him. Something austere, something integral about these mosaics.' I was not aware of course that 20th century modernism was also drawn to this two dimensional symbolic art, the flat picture plane.

But I also responded to some Renaissance painters. I liked Giorgione: 'unshackled himself from a religious theme, thus giving greater freedom for integrity.' I also took to Mantegna's St Sebastian: 'has God given his body a purity before resurrection?' But later art of the Counter-Reformation left questions: 'is the Mystery solved by the transcendental suffering of Christ?' Yet I was moved by Titian's Assumption in the Frari and came round to Tintoretto 'even if I can feel little enthusiasm for him'. I verbalised a clash between the role of religion and an aesthetic approach: 'if I prefer my churches clean, will I reject the finery of a Tintoretto, Veronese, Tiepolo?' At his stage I turned away from the Baroque. Later it became a favourite art form.

More than any other painter I was drawn to Carpaccio, those extraordinary narrative paintings in the Scuola di San Giorgio degli Schiavoni. I'll just put down my thoughts. 'Is this the answer to Spender's the Creative Element? It does fulfil the demand of having a focal point. The monks move away from St Jerome and the Basilisk like a flight of doves scurrying into the sky above the Piazza San Marco. It is an achievement of reality. This is the core of existence. And there is a tremendous amount of thought put into its component parts as colour. Consider St Jerome. The combination of red and pale green.' Again: 'Religion is natural, made approachable for man. Here is the light of salvation. It is finely toned. No vulgar luminescence. Moments of eternity are set in natural surroundings.' Of his Annunciation in the Ca d'Oro: 'the classical archways keep the painting in absolute control. This is a moment of stillness, a timeless presence of the Eternal.' On all future visits to Venice I always revisited the Scuola.

That return journey opened up comparisons between Rome, Florence and Venice. In my first visit to Rome, those dramatic sites, the classical of the Forum, the Pantheon, the Colosseum, the Renaissance and Baroque Vatican, the Piazzas such as Novara, the portentous memorial to Victor Emmanuel, all impressed, but I was never to warm to Rome. On this second visit I was taken by Bernini, seeing his strength in capturing the drama of the particular moment, but also the way the spiritual became degraded into the sensual. His statues of course graced the wonderful Piazza Novara. But I felt defeated by Rome. St Peter's just seemed ponderous: 'even the gentle pathos of Michelangelo's Pieta is overpowered by its massive columns. Bernini's statues failed to humanise the enormous Godly nave: it's a city of sober grace but I failed to respond to its spirit.' Even a performance of Verdi's *Aida* at the Baths of Caracalla was mere 'cinemascope': it lacked the human. Several later visits did not change this response, though I came to appreciate some of it fine Baroque churches.

En route to Florence we first visited the marvellous hill town of Orvieto, with its black and white cathedral and those brazen frescoes of the Last Judgment by Luca Signorelli. I'm not sure how positively I reacted to the frescoes in the Basilica in Assisi. Of those by Petro Lorenzetti I write: 'it's as if the artist has caught these persons in momentary distraction from spiritual contemplation'. Am I here describing the Giottos?: 'each component character could stand on his own as a work of sculpture. They do not exist for one another but in their own right. There is nothing liquid and fluent about these frescoes. Their unity lies in the interplay of the strength of the eyes; compare Donne's metaphor of the stringing together of eye-balls.' Had I failed to recognise in Giotto the beginnings of Renaissance humanism? Or was I regretting the breach from the primitives?

And so to Florence. We stayed in a youth hotel in Fiesole. I wondered if the city, with the views of the Arno, the Piazza Vecchio, might indeed replace Venice in my affections. The painter I liked best was Fra Angelico. The breakthrough in Florentine art lay in its discovery of perspective, Uccello the obvious example, and a new emphasis on structural form over Byzantine character. I engaged in a debate between the Flemish and the Florentine, the former with its cult of realism and truth, the latter its cult of beauty. 'Religion', I argued, 'requires expression through the cult of realism and is in danger of becoming decadent in the cult of beauty.' Whenever a Florentine like Filippo Lippi borrowed from the Flemish, he lost the transcendental beauty of a Botticelli: where a Flemish such as Memling became indebted to the Florentine, his art was weakened. I was on safer ground in my intuition that Florentine art was an expression of Plato's ideas of Absolute Form, a focus on Ethics and the need for Goodness, Humility, Courage rather than on Christianity itself. I still seem to defend the need for art to have something to convey, a message, and am still no convert to Art for Art's Sake.

I was not to be won over by German art on the last lap of this journey, its 'starkness of expression'. I preferred the stripped down churches over the baroque. But I enjoyed the rather kitsch Romantic Way. My favourite memory is of a kind German in Augsburg cathedral taking pity on me, still in my Mediterranean summer clothes in the chilly German autumn, and giving me his overcoat.

But at the end of this journal for 1957 there is a possible change in outlook. I was now reading Bernard Berenson (today so discredited). He off-sets the decorative against the illustrative, the former seemingly opening up Art for Art's Sake, the latter art with an ulterior motive. Was I wobbling?: 'is it inevitable that artistic and religious tastes should be the same?' Was I still wedded to a version of Spender: 'I believe in the core of life. I don't know what that has to do with Christianity. It seems very Platonist to me.' In the end I sit on the fence: 'maybe it all depends on your personality, whether you're more of an artist or more of a religious.' But I move away from Berenson's emphasis on the tactile, the body over the soul. I see the tactile as constraining the artist's spiritual expression: 'consider El Greco. Here the spiritual invades the heart. Why do we need to search for tactile values? They are not needed. With El Greco an emotional grasp suffices.' Yet I do support the outlook of Berenson and Ernest Newman that western art presents a human life cycle: 'that is why modern artists are so fascinating. The uses and abuses of maturity.' And I now rally to those moderns, Matisse and Shostakovitch, who break away from the classical: 'relying on their intellectual strength to fashion work in progress. Theirs is a greater belief in emotional intensity, less in structural harmony.' Was I anticipating my reading of Nietzsche with his preference for the Dionysiac over the Apollonian?: 'yet I believe the moderns would never stand up if it were not for a considerable self-discipline and grasp of classical principles.'

The very last entry is on Dostoyevsky, opening up a debate on the role of genius. Should genius be licensed for an unbridled pursuit of the Absolute or should there be limits? Here my historical sense came into play, for if all values are subject to cultural change, then by definition there can be no claim for total freedom. Genius has to have bounds. Or was I just saying, whether or not there is absolute freedom-and the existentialists say there is - it is just too dangerous to pursue? So by what values should we act? 'Christianity says the reality is in the action. If you search for freedom through the practical realisation of your ideals, freedom will be won by their implementation.' Those who pursue absolute freedom betray the claims of society and their own reality. I still seem to have my feet on the ground as I faced Oxford.

I have mentioned various friends along the way in this chapter. I was very fortunate in National Service in finding the friends I'd largely failed to find at school. Three stand out, Michael Williams, Rashid (then Patrick) Maxwell, Robert Tollemache. I met Michael on joining up at Victoria Barracks in October 1955 and our naval careers ran parallel, though he stayed on in the minesweeper fleet and had a far tougher time than I. Rashid I met in Malta. Robert I met at Suez. All three of us were struggling through identity crises: Michael to discover if his vocation was as an artist: Rashid in dealing with an appalling authoritarian banker Father and likewise seeking artistic outlets and the religious: Robert, seemingly rather aloof, but searching for a life time role. I think it was this shared confusion of purpose that drew us together.

8
UNDERGRADUATE: WORCESTER COLLEGE 1957-60

Usually undergraduates at Oxbridge matriculate at the age of 18 and encounter the University at a highly impressionable age. I suspect that accounts for the sentimental regard in which most students look back on their university. By coming up later at 20 through National Service I was always to be less sentimental about Oxford. Keith Thomas has recorded his wish that once he'd reached the paradise of Oxford after his National Service he determined never to leave. But I have no such romantic recollection of Oxford as an undergraduate. There was always going to be little continuity between my exposure to a variety of social life in the Navy and the far more restricted elitist life of Oxford. This was compounded by the still predominantly Public School intake of Worcester College, though the admissions don, David Mitchell, was working on a gradual transformation of the college through a larger state school entry into a more academically minded college. One of the leading Etonians of my year christened this grammar school entry, 'the grey men'. As it happened, there was to be a disjuncture between the kind of intellectual enquiry I was pursuing during National Service and the academic demands of the Oxford School of History. I had some status in the College as its senior scholar in History of my year, but I was far from confident in my academic skills. Still, I was respected as an intellectual and tried to carry forward my interests in culture and religion into Oxford life.

Provost at the time was John Masterman. He was almost invisible except at occasional sherry parties. I did not know at the time of his continuing role in intelligence and of his recruitment for the M15 and M16. For reasons that will be obvious, I was never to be approached. An alumnus of the college once volunteered himself for the promotion of an Indian-based journal of which I was co-editor, *The Indo-British Review*, and, indeed, was to act on its behalf both in London and India. But I only realised later that he did so as a screen for carrying out intelligence work in India. Seeing him scything down high grass in his garden in Kent, I realised I knew nothing about him, and was so distressed by his deceit that I broke off all relationships. Masterman had been active in the Double Cross system, though Tom Bower in his book on this counter-espionage claims Masterman greatly exaggerated his role, and also faulted him for the way he had found ways round the rules on privacy to publish his own version. I always saw Masterman as the paradigmatic *éminence grise*, one who would advise on the appointment of the Regius Professor of History - in fact his former pupil Hugh Trevor Roper - one who went on to be Vice-Chancellor.

I found academic history tricky. Many NS men found it hard anyway to get back into the 'A' level rhythm of study. During National Service I'd all but neglected history, apart from the history of music and painting. In the prelims course, the Age of Bede, I had to address such particular questions as Anglo-Saxon place names, legal systems, coinage, a level of detail that the positivist Oxford School of History emphasised. I was happier with Europe in the Age of Expansion, for here I was genuinely excited by the history of the conquistadors, and here lay the origins of my interest in the history of Mission. I recall writing a long essay on the Jesuit mission to the Spanish Americas. But I was lucky in my college tutors. The mediaeval historian, James Campbell, one of Keith Mcfarlane's gifted students, joined the college the same year. Somehow the fact that he was but three years older never came into my mind. Here was a quality of academicism I felt I had to match, and, ever afterwards in the degree, I concentrated on mediaeval history. Rumour has it that he was already teaching the Age of Bede as an undergraduate, but surely that cannot be true? He was seriously short-sighted which makes his extensive archival scholarship all the more remarkable. Harry Pitt was the Modern History tutor and it was widely recognised that the two formed a famous friendship and were admirable foils as teachers. James taught me to address detail but with lively occasional references to the present. Harry insisted on tough reasoning but also risked quite impossible generalisations. He walked with a limp, thought to be a war wound from the Normandy landings. Much later he told me it was from a car crash following a bibulous evening in the mess. I was mortified when Harry tweaked my scholar's gown at the beginning of the Lent term, and in consequence, in my notes the name Python Pitt headed his excellent lectures on European expansion. Later I learnt he did so to every first year history scholar.

I was to pass prelims but at the time I was far from sure if I wanted to continue with History, was attracted to PPP, Physiology, Psychology, Philosophy, and blurted all this out to James. He dispatched me to Harry and David Mitchell. These were revealing conversations. Harry had been inspired by Toynbee at Haileybury and was himself to be seriously disappointed by Oxford history. To quote him from my diary: 'With the collapse of liberal values it is impossible to pass moral judgements in history, to state that John was a good or bad king, to believe that the west is the best civilisation. The mental outlook that has come to replace liberalism is honest doubt. That is why the Oxford School of History is so academic, and if you regard it in this way, will see it as dried-up. You will not find answers for life today in the study of history, nor indeed in any subject at Oxford, except possibly Theology.' I reflected that he had come to see Toynbeeism as history distorted into theory. Harry continued: 'Toynbeeism's main historical interest lay in its wealth of information. He postulated that his own aim in teaching history was the ordering of the mind into a disciplined and analytical approach.' David Mitchell also emphasised that the aim of studying history was clear-sightedness, the ability to concentrate on a certain theme without deviation and with cogent argument. Neither offered any prospect that Oxford philosophy would meet my needs. Mine were speculative, Oxford philosophy analytical. Mitchell doubted that Oxford would solve my problems. All Oxford offered was intellectual discipline.

All this was discouraging. But I realise now PPP would have been a huge mistake. Its Psychology was mere behaviourism, based on rats. I found this reply to Harry which may be I never sent.

> 'Dear Mr Pitt,
>
> I tried to get in touch with a psychologist at Cambridge but failed to do so. But I have made up my mind to continue reading History. I think a wrong attitude to it on my part to a certain extent blinded me to the real merits of reading History. So I must thank you for your helpful, illuminating and rather depressing advice.'

Thoughts on a holiday in Greece over the first summer vacation 1958 do not indicate much progress: 'what I am really seeking is a kind of emotional involvement with my work. The misfortune of Oxford history is I have to frame for myself a non-emotional picture. But after laying the foundation I should be able to relive historical characters in much the same way as Cavafy did the decadent characters of the dying Roman Empire.'

Possibly though on the same holiday this reflection, in terms of matching the pragmatic demands of Oxford history, was more positive: 'I somehow feel over the last month I have come to a definite decision to sacrifice the romantic for the scholastic. It is absurd to think that the latter necessarily kills the former. It is possible to be learned without losing sensibility.'

But I never fully engaged with History as an undergraduate though I worked hard enough. I suspect I was always, as my Cambridge examiners had detected, going in the wrong direction. There are a few comments in the journals: 'Maybe History is valuable after all. I have merely been too sceptical.' Campbell encouraged me to work on what interested me. I was taken by Celtic civilisation, vowed hard to look at Russian history. 'Marxism is a rejection of the Middle Ages - of the attempt to make God the ruling agent of the world.' 'Is History a God? Do I commit myself to an inherent plan in History, so denying myself negative freedom? If there are rules, am I free if I distrust the development and fulfilment of those rules? Or are there no rules and no directions? Is History meaningless but for the threat of its apocalyptic end?' 'I may distrust its empiricism at the expense of general principles but I am ready to see it as an art form, in the manner of Berenson's estimate of humanism. This value alone raises History to one of the most educational of studies. But can it be didactic?' 'So often you have a feeling of detachment in reading History, a compulsory impartiality - you long to escape from this prison of detachment - you can do so by surrendering yourself to the sense of growth and change in historical movement - something created, false, but involving you in history. And there is biography, opening up an existential insight into the life and ideals of other men.'

The conclusion is a bit confused. 'And yet if you really believed in History you would renounce all search for the absolute, all desire for the absolute, a search for the same in all other reading, such as the novel of sensibility or existentialist philosophy, and concentrate on some all embracing commitment with History, for some experience which would involve the discovery of new symbols and of a newly conceived absolute.' Do I detect the continuing impact here of Berdyaev but a corrective from Isaiah Berlin? 'It is easy to convert History into a Christian framework. Maybe Marxist history is but a fantastic acceptance of man's original sin as the primary motive force but with this exceptional difference: instead of driving him into hell it is leading him to the communist paradise.'

In fact my preoccupations still lay with religion and high culture. Questions of belief feature straightaway at Worcester. My first journal entry at Oxford reads: 'So now it is beginning, the long intense conversations with fellow scholars. The first few days saw my fellow freshmen terrified of talking, embarking on factual conversations with an inevitable *cul-de-sac*. But tonight we talked, Steve Radcliffe, John Gretton, Alastair Morton. And we talked on belief, though failing to differentiate between Christ and God, but discussing why we do or do not believe in God. Maybe it is no more than a state of awareness, a response to religion akin to our response to music, both to be explained in physiological terms. And God should be open to intellectual defence. My own conclusion: "I am certain that man is yet still incapable of an intellectual proof of God, even if God is the Hegelian idea. We must still rely on our intuition and feelings." But if this emotional access is closed, how else can we pull down that barrier except by rational argument? Evangelism is surely like banging your head against a brick wall. John Osborne and Colin Wilson were somehow in this conversation.'

In fact religious enquiry was to feature prominently in year one and two. Michael Williams and I used to attend services or meetings at all the various religious institutions, a kind of cafeteria approach. It kept the enquiry alive but led to no conclusions. Searching for answers I visited the Rev O'Brien, but all he did was send me away with a list of bible readings, and I suspect that killed off any response I ever had to the evangelical literalist approach. I was very excited by a visit to Campion Hall at the invitation of the Jesuit Peter Hebblethwaite. There I met Peter Levi, possibly the most exciting person I met as an undergraduate in Oxford: 'spoke with an alarming staccato voice, at tangents, and yet with excitement. The poetic intellect is NOT logical.' But I was not tempted by Catholicism, may be the Maltese model had put me off. I was impressed by a Quaker meeting. I was still being advised by George Silver who visited me in the college: 'George is earnest and unaffected in his faith as ever.'

Was I drawn to Greek orthodoxy? A highlight of my holiday in Greece and Turkey in the first summer vacation was a visit to Mt Athos. This is a bit of a detour. To quote from the diary I kept 15th August 1958 onwards: 'Scenery very beautiful, strange that our ascetics should choose so beautiful a site. Always in view the Holy Mountain Athos, growing as the day grew old, a fine stone monument in the sky'. So to the first monastery, Daphni. 'Taken inside, along white undecorated corridors, to the dining room, there greeted by splendid jolly monks who benignly handed us large bowls of soup and great chunks of brown bread. Glorious view from the balcony. Fine singing of the litany, the Bible read with an abominable speed, however.' Next was Karys. 'Heavily bitten in the night, woke at two to the shattering sound of the bells for office.' 'Met a charming eremitical monk in the morning. Gave me grapes and figs from his sizeable garden. His house an extraordinary collection of paintings and prints, most of them of a very popular nature.' Next was Vatopedi: 'along chequered paths of sunlight and shades of tree, passing the autumn of golden topped branches, stopping to feast ourselves on blackberries and the yellow ripened figs and then staggering down a path of soot - a recent fire had raged over the hillside - down to Vatopedi.' 'Up early to go to liturgy. In a way enjoyable, centring round the two entrances, one of the Gospel, the other of the consecrated bread, a constant flow of litanies. Some of the monks clearly found the office amusing, and I sensed a lack of true devotion here. But the church grew on me as time went on and I began to delight in the play of light on the brass candelabra. After the service, formal breakfast in the state rooms, with crystallised marmalade and water, then coffee. Very quiet and formal.'

Then by boat, and an arduous walk through the hills, towards Lavra: 'After a swim on again, with Athos changing every step from a stone lion to a more amiable green covered mountain, the joy of arrival. A short little monk was our host, placing an enormous dish of macaroni before us and red wine. Then sleep, overlooking the inlet of Lavra, the sea edging the rocks with white foam.' Lavra seems to have been most memorable for the arrival of a

Danish ballet dancer, seducing monks all the way: 'the attractive sibilant lisps, eyes glazed, a pretty reflection of light and no more, the shutters permanently down. The ideal face for a ballet dancer, high well defined cheek bones with a marked but not over-defined prominent brow. It lends him the appearance of being made up, even now.' A spear fisherman later made overtures of love to him, tickling his ear and pinching his neck. There was an extraordinary monk who had prophesied world war in 1956, that Germany would be orthodox by 1961 and Turkey half orthodox. Then a tough walk, mountaineering in fact, together with the ballet dancer, en route to Ayios Paulus. Luckily, we met a half undressed forester on the way, who gave us a meal of beans and potatoes: 'a most friendly fellow, stuck here amongst his timber mules, harness, pots and pans and water can, babbling merrily of the war against the Germans and the supreme indifference to it all of the British.' He steered us away from a fruitless climb of Athos itself and so I proceeded on my own, struggling through ferns and brambles, often losing sight of the path, till the monastery was in sight, 'retreating into the mountain but looking in fine condition and well protected by its lower and crenelated wall.' 'I was first greeted by a most friendly monk. He spoke English and chatted of the Englishmen he had met, of the English books he possessed, all the while feeding me with melon and grapes and ouzo. I was invited to read the story of the Transfiguration. He had been to America for six years, working in a car factory, then making shells during the war, till, tired of it all, he returned to be a priest in

Cephalonia.' He had been in the monastery now for three years.

In fact the monks were to be very hostile, bombarding me with pamphlets on EOKA, on Makarios being behind bars, 'one of the greatest crimes of our century'. Quotations from Churchill, Bevin and Compton Mackenzie, 'those who praised us in the past but now accuse us.' In the morning I was to be harassed all over again and all but pushed out of the monastery, such hostility merely bringing out the colonialist in me. Still, I then met up again with my friendly monk, 'his conversation a little flagging but his generosity unbounded. His arms had many sores, his feet bunions, toe nails mere strips, yet padding about his house, caring for his garden, reading his holy books, the true man of faith. He showed me round the monastery in the afternoon.' Then away across a rough path to Dionysiou, 'perched gull-like over the sea, with a friendly welcome, almost over-friendly, from the guest-master.' Spent three days there before returning, very sea sick, to the mainland.

I doubt if there was any religious epiphany on Athos. I wrote of a failure of contemplation. But this was my first exposure to monasticism. I may not have realised at the time just how depressed these Athos communities be, their recruitment from the Orthodox states of Eastern Europe all but dried up under Soviet occupation. But I was ever afterwards drawn to monasticism, so its influence was considerable.

There was one small victory for freedom of worship. Worcester had compulsory chapel and for failure to attend you would be fined. You could get someone to sign you in but if the fraud was discovered, a fine followed. A group of us protested and went to the Provost. Meekly Masterman backed down and attendance became voluntary. In fact I liked the college chapel, with its vaguely Byzantine feel. I also attended chapels of other colleges such as New to hear their choirs.

In fact my interests remained far more focussed on cultural issues. Painting was giving way to literature and poetry. Before going up I went to a number of exhibitions. I found Monet 'skin-deep: Monet is a painter of dissolution, of one element melting into another.' He compared poorly with Cezanne: 'always searched for the inscape of his subject.' I was now more impressed than earlier by Matisse: 'he insists on an artistic unity for his poetic intuition.' I found form too superficial in Modigliani.

I doubt if I was aware of all the debates on Modernism in literature. I'd discovered Virginia Woolf. 'Heavens, how does Woolf do it, this permanent intense awareness of the interesting side of ordinary events and dull people.' But the poverty of my literary taste is betrayed by an almost equal excitement over the ongoing publication of Lawrence Durrell's *The Alexandria Quartet*.

I was moving away from social art to art for art's sake and in that sense turning modernist. 'It is simply a question that if the artist concerned himself with the social scene as a social problem, he is in danger of staking everything on a particular issue and, in the event of a Swedish state, leaving himself with no alternative other than creating inert reflections of social excellence. (How did I square this with the cinema of Bergman?') 'It is permissible, though, to treat social problems as art, commenting on them as an artist e.g. Velasquez, Goya and not as a politician.' Not quite a declaration of art for art's sake but close: 'It is clearly necessary to separate aesthetics from metaphysics. Aesthetics should be the study of artistic method. It is because they have been confused that 1) art as craft has become despised 2) art has been disastrously associated with philosophical ideas. We regard a painting no longer for its technical genius but for its meaning.'

But a caveat: 'remember that modern art, because there are no common standards, technique can only be assessed on its ability to express the very personal ideas of the artist. Can we confidently state what those ideas be?'

I was the art representative on the JCR committee and was to buy at least one very good painting, a John Wells, from the new Bear Lane Art gallery. This was the origin of a major life-time friendship with Elizabeth Deighton.

And poetry and being a poet remained central. I'd discovered Rilke, surely our greatest modern poet. The first ever book I reviewed, for a student paper, at the invitation of Henry Kamen, was Butler's study of Rilke. At the same time I was reading Hegel's Aesthetics. This accounts for the following statement: 'I am convinced that the poetical mind precedes the philosophical. I find this is always so with myself and what I have perceived through poetic intuition may not be recognised by my rationalising mind till years later. One is never wrong in poetry. One is possibly incomprehensible or else only partly right.' Some of the poetry I wrote is in an appendix.

I was as always preoccupied with personal friendship. Here is one entry: 'Is friendship altruistic and mutual? Does the purely self-reliant person, which may be hypothetical, regard friendship as an entertainment, thus vulgarising it? Does not friendship assume glory when it satisfies mutual needs and when it is given to satisfy the need of the other without thinking of personal need?'

One friend was Andrew Baring. Here was a brilliant but self-destructive personality. He was one Worcester friend who invited me to visit his home. It amazes me in retrospect that he never saw through the rather odd circumstances of his Mother living in genteel poverty, only to learn later, from an inheritance he came into at 21, that he was illegitimate. It was to shatter his self-confidence. One of my first recorded conversations was on Wittgenstein, our looking at the world through a picture frame, formulated as a Euclidean theory. Why not see the world, Andrew proposed, without a frame? He took this significantly further. Why not admit we have no soul: 'my own seemingly petty escape into reality through self-analysis seen as a quite inadequate assertion of the experience of the soul.' Andrew, however, did not at this stage retreat into nihilism. He still saw merit in the study of individual works of art, in empiricism. But he was hard to take: 'how can I tolerate his endless chatter over pieces of china, Victorian lamp stands and Baxter prints?' Andrew was very critical of my own introspection: 'the etherealizing remote intellectual ivory tower, Copley, is incapable of relating ideas to human beings.' Possibly more to the point: 'I will never think "positively" in company. I willingly state hypotheses. It is as if I were afraid of criticism of my ideals.'

Later, now 12 November 1958, Andrew set out to destroy the very idea of personality: 'experiences pass over us, they cannot be focussed and given significance by our "self"', he declared. 'You see everything in a narrow area of experience which I call "self", rather than allowing this self-justifying area to be broken up into some strange pantheistic mood. You cut yourself off from all ugly contaminating experience.'

A year later, 23 November 1959, by now suicidal, Andrew unsparingly looked at himself: 'how to accept the man who cannot live in accordance with truth, whose whole personality is based on a lie to protect himself from the recognition that he is of bastard birth.' Having destroyed that adolescent self-deception, 'from there it was a neurotic search for a kind of standing in society, an endless tussle between acrid recrimination and deep despair at the hopelessness of it all. How to love his Mother in the light of her deception, how to establish a different relationship, find alternative mother figures?' But that would fail: 'he loved them not for themselves but for the way they could restore a belief in his own shattered persona.' It was all a hopeless quest and he came to despise himself. Here was an extraordinary confession. The diary continues: 'his feelings drove him back to the moment of severance from all that he had ever known of security and belief in himself. To recover that security had once led him into an infinite game of make-belief and tragic self-deception. It led him into pathological lying. The conflict was unbearable, for it did nothing to satisfy the brilliant quality of unprincipled intellect and intense dissatisfied energy. Hatred, indiscriminate and revengeful, alternated with sudden spurts of ludicrous ambition. Moments of self-delusion as to his greatness gave way to a recognition of his "palsied self". He knew that the real self was utterly adrift and had no confidence or belief in itself.' How, I wondered, could Andrew survive such self-contempt: 'see your own body deteriorate into death, a slow curdling of the blood.' I offered religious contemplation or psychiatry as the way out: 'accept the slow destruction of your false world as you come to recognise the only possible self which is your painful reality'. And, in fact, all this was but a reflection of my own painful predicament.

But Andrew did not commit suicide. He gave away all his inheritance as tainted. He got a 4th in Finals but somehow persuaded, a few years later, the Leonhard brothers to take him on for the MA in Anthropology. He gave them a hard time. Later he trained as a French polisher, went into the antique trade and lived in the beautiful village of Bradford-on-Avon. There he made a considerable nuisance of himself, and died quite young. I lost all contact after leaving Worcester.

There was the same excitement in making a friend from another college as at school from another house. My friend was Norman Coles from Balliol. I cannot recall how we met. He introduced me to the blind Ved Mehta, then a student at Balliol. You would never have known he was blind. I have to say of all my friends that I asked home he was the least liked by my Father and step-mother. He came straight from an Aldermaston march and this was hardly likely to impress my Father. He joined us in my second year in April 1959 for a reading party in Cornwall at Port Quin. I wrote: 'merely listening to Norman Coles talking compels me to admit to my "reasoning" incompetence. He is so well grounded in common sense and sound association of ideas.' I saw him as someone all too ready to surrender romantic or idealist attitudes to come into line with the cautious, sceptical approach of the Oxford philosopher. He would never allow any vicious element in a character to sway him into a perverse sympathy. He judged character by a strict morality. I was surprised when he declared: 'Tony, I think I am going to like you after all.' At the heart of his morality was his Roman Catholicism. The quality he demanded most of people was a correct estimate of their talents: 'an over-estimation is sinful, proud.' (Compare this to Bertrand Russell's condemnation of the same trait on the different grounds that it leads to unhappiness.) But this did not restrict Norman's breadth of understanding. My observation: 'indeed it is arguable that once a man has established a central philosophy it becomes far easier to entertain a variety of ideas. It is only the man who is struggling for a certainty of faith who will be minded to blind himself to alternatives.'

Norman got a First in PPE and went on to take, at the same time as myself, a B.Phil in Philosophy, the indispensable training in those days to be a University teacher. He took up a post at TCD. Much later he made the national news for seemingly being lost on a coastal path. I fear here was another person I lost all contact with in my third year.

There were other friends. In my first year I was close to Simon Brown and we went on holiday together to Greece in the summer of 1958. Of my friends I asked home - in this case I think for my 21st - Simon was by far the most appealing. He charmed my step-mother, and Father must have sensed the acumen of a legal brain of a future Lord Justice. Simon changed from History to Law after Prelims and seemingly decided that all metaphysical questions were not him. We drifted apart. The academic calibre of College was much enhanced by Fulbright and Rhodes scholars. I did not get to know Lloyd Weinreb, but did in time become a close friend of future Stanford Professor of English literature, Ron Rebholz. For two years we were in adjacent college rooms but only afterwards became friends. Rhodes scholar, Alastair Morton, later Chairman of the Channel Tunnel project and sadly at the cost of an early death, was a tough conversationalist. Charles Nunn, fellow History scholar, was a good academic foil, invited me to his home in Tiverton, went on to an academic career in Economics at the University of Alberta. I gather he dropped out and ran a small-holding. He died young. Others I knew and liked, Tobias Rodgers, Robin Wright, were both likewise to die young. John Gretton was a fellow intellectual, sought out the fashionable and was taught philosophy by Iris Murdoch, went on to be a political activist on behalf of the Moroccan Polisario front, yet another early death. I wrote this strange entry in the diary at the time: 'Gretton wants to be a writer. I note the ruthless ugly gaze in his eyes and he occasionally reaches beyond effeminate gestures and sloppy uneducated statements into an unperceived sense of purpose. I tell him he must acquire a quality of fanaticism.' Later, there was a terrifying conflict between John and Charles over the incredibly beautiful Joanna Booker. Maybe I enjoyed college life more than I realise.

The one person I did not get to know was Perry Anderson. He held the same Open Fletcher scholarship in History from the year before. He chose to read Modern Languages rather than History, recognising how out of sympathy he would be with its positivist approach. He sat with us on the scholars table but did not converse. I saw him as a *narodnik* and have been haunted by the thought of him all my life. Years later, we were in the same guesthouse at Queen's, Belfast to attend Eric Hobsbawn's Wiles lectures on Nationalism. One night, much the worse for wear, he burst into my room by mistake. I fled the next day to my friends, David and Hilary Harkness. I had occasion to respond to his irresponsible but provocative essays on Modern India in the LRB, though my reply was only to be published in *Gandhi Marg*. If Anderson was too terrifying to know, I did get to know and like Quentin Hoare, his later joint editor of *New Left Review*. I visited Quentin's Mother's home in Sandwich.

Did I fall under the spell of Oxford? I had this to say of a walk from Christ Church meadows, down the Isis to Magdalen. 'A grey haze seems to carpet the pale green fields, the grey of time-toned grey statuary. This was not the artificial beauty of the Cambridge backs, but something more natural, more free. I really did enjoy the walk, watching the precision of the oarsmen, punters in the logged channels, the autumn leaves strewn in the unkempt undergrowth. Eventually to Magdalen and the deer, alert and frail in the park.' Port Meadow was another pleasing walk. There I always imagined in the distance the dark riders of Mordor. Tolkien at the time took over my imagination. Even so, journeys outside of Oxford gave me more pleasure.

Following Prelims I made my first visit to Paris, Pete Smith from University College my guide. Astonishingly, I slept through till 4pm the next day, so exhausted had I become. We stayed in the Hotel de Normandie in the heart of the Latin Quarter. 'Oh yes, the strangest thing of all, the tramps, huddled asleep, on the pavement. Just a pair of feet to reveal the man, head trussed up in a sleeping bag.' The next day, 'the most fabulous view the length of the Triumphal way'. I took to the book stalls on the Seine, though all I bought was a book on Primitive Masks, the beginning of an obsessive buying of masks on foreign travels. The glaring whiteness of Sacré-Coeur in the light of the unexpected Parisian sun. The glass of the Sainte-Chapelle. Rather priggishly I wrote of my experience of *La Traviata* (extraordinarily one could just turn up and get a ticket): 'whether the experience of emotion had any progressive element, leading to an Idea, I could not say', but I was much moved. Much taken by a Greek orthodox service. I wanted to strip the Gothic from the Romanesque in Notre Dame. Paris at the time was in the grip of the Algerian crisis; 'soldiers moving through the Latin quarter with guns at the ready, but the crowd just absorbed it all, disinterested.' I did wonder if the woman who ran the hotel was another Madame Desfarges and the hotel was a centre of Algerian intrigue. I went to an exhibition on Saharan art, 8th century BC, on the penetration into the Sahara by the Mycenaean. The École Militaire inspired the thought that the artist should always be in revolt: 'for art can sink so soon from serenity into complacency.'

I had some exciting meetings. A Canadian at the Cité Universitaire, 'almost certainly queer'. There was a weird encounter with a drunk American in Les Halles. I had to keep pulling up his trousers, all the while walking through the market and so back to his hotel and his girl-friend, the reason for his drunkenness. He was also full of his failure to write a play in the style of Noel Coward.

Some random thoughts in Paris. 'Self-discipline is the ability to stick to a policy carefully deliberated. You are purely the judge of that policy. Sin is the failure to live up to its standards.' And then, given that I'd decided to stick with History, this promising observation: 'History may serve one vital function. The temptation for the modern psychiatrist or philosopher is to generalise from the much degraded modern mankind. History should furnish the more enquiring brain with more inspiring examples.'

I discovered the wilderness landscape of Northumberland through the kind invitation of Richard Rowlatt to stay on his granny's farm outside Hexham. I tried to do justice to the experience. Here for example, on burning off the stubble: 'drawing flaming sticks along the spent brown tufts of grass and seeing the wind furiously drive the fire up the hillside. Extraordinary to see the roarers ahead of the smoke, haggling with the wall which it could not overshoot. A kind of fire ritual. Sense of the fire god. A Forster short story.' Then there was the Wall: 'we stopped off at Winshields, the highest point at 1,230 feet, walking across a sodden stretch of heath to hit the wall at a segment of original mortar. The great volcanic rock range. It really is a noticeable barrier, an ideal frontier, and the wall does indeed clutch at the most inaccessible hills.' But I saw all this description as a false romanticism, my trying to see the moor through the eyes of a Catherine Earnshaw or Heathcliff. 'My eyes are blinded by insincere adjectives. Strip it all away, remove all the accretions of centuries. See it with scientific accuracy.'

Was this any better?: 'Our journey to Rothbury. Climbing the hill and making heavy weather and reaching the segment of what was really a plateau. Amazing to avoid the main swirl of a rainstorm curving the sky from north to east in grey shivers of lines, ending with the hail hitting our backs as we climbed down. Then the sky incandescent on the horizon with a white heat of sunset, more dazzling than the beech hedges and the silk-tasselled larches, the extraordinary sense of jumping on the hill and feeling it quake.'

Then there was the challenge of describing the fierce Cornish coastline at Port Quin. It had been a reading party overshadowed by the fear that one of the party was suicidal. We watched his comings and goings with dread. 'This is how I should like to have seen ourselves in the Cornish landscape. I wanted to see ourselves as the dislocated and lame of the world, the philosopher, the artist, the poet, confronted with our wounded bodies, seeking some way of recovery both for ourselves and for society. I'd like to see ourselves searching for some empathy with the elemental sounds of the wind and sea. There was one vision of conflicting armies, of the Mongol Tartars sweeping in continual charge of waves upon the shielded crusaders of the rocks. A sense of the sea as a relentless force with endless reservoirs of destructivity. The other vision was of the great downward curving slab of rock, either the predatory swoop of the eagle or else a diabolical monster swallowing up the entrance of hell. Somewhat like those crude beasts in Macedonian art in the paintings of Mount Athos.'

If these were images of destruction there were some of trance and dream. I clearly saw the night-darkened inlet of Port Quin, 'melting between the velvet blackness of the rocks into the night sky. But the darkness was softened by a band of soft whiteness in the sky, the pale reflection of moonlight on low flying clouds. This night-time dream image, something like a Paul Nash painting, recalled the daytime reality of myself sitting on the rocks beside the noise of the sea grinding the pebbles. The striking difference between the day vision and the night was the sense of the extensive distance of the limbs of rocks, groping far into the sea.'

One reason for looking back at the past is to try and see where I was before the trauma, was there in fact a major hiatus in my life, was I developing in a far more interesting way than I was to do afterwards? Or was I heading towards a *cul-de-sac*?

Maybe there was the same old issue of sincerity, of authenticity? I'd picked up a piece by the poet Horowitz in *Isis* on Oxford Attitudes on going up. 'We hide behind our self-defences, fail to pull down the destructive barrier and open ourselves to a genuine interest in people and ideas.' I feel this to be a ghastly and truthful analysis of myself.'

Intellectually, the tension lay between rational analysis and intuition. How compatible was the current academic project with being a poet?: 'to struggle for clarity and reason is to destroy poetry.' Rilke was a huge influence. 'I wonder if Rilke did not populate the realm of death with angels to humanise the terrifying search for a seemingly incommunicable absolute.'

'Rilke's concept of the animal moving with supreme unawareness of death. The child living within the pure realm of death, unconscious of any separation between life and death.'

Auden was another major influence: 'we must surrender our dreams of Eden and realise our real fulfilment lies in the rational understanding of the laws of Jerusalem.' I was reading his *The Sea and the Mirror*: 'a resolution that a poem should be inspired by a genuine not an imagined experience. How to connect a recognition of suffering with a wish to explore and condemn it?'

Was there continuity with my earlier commitment to the social and political? 'Do I have to be a social being? Or can I not justify my existence within the remote existentialist world of solitude? Can I exclude the force of politics, the threat of global extinction?'

Listening to a speech by Trevor Huddleston: 'I disagree that race is the primary issue of the world. Our issue is that of the uncertainty of our values. Or is the Toynbee thesis the real issue? The need to realise the common threads of world religions in an effort to arrive at a spiritual weapon to combat Communism?'

The diary suggests an impasse. 'I seem to be enduring a kind of claustrophobia brought on by a sense of my shortcomings.' 'I have grown so unpractised in being myself that I am shy when I say those things I really feel.' 'I am most shy with my family, for here I am far more conscious of the barriers that state our difference.'

I recorded during the Cornish holiday a conversation with Michael. 'Intriguing that he should have struck on that very quality of mind that I am most afraid of. That is my laziness. A refusal to apply a penetrating analysis to accumulated knowledge.' (The very quality I had in fact to show as an academic historian.) 'I raised the idea of surrendering one's life to a cause. Michael suggested, as an alternative, the life of experience but for its creative expression in art.' 'But I am terrified of insufficiency of character to stand up to the demands of that way of life. And the sense of inadequacy must stem, Michael suggests, from a lack of anything to say.'

Early in Trinity term 1959 came the trauma.

9
SURVIVING TRAUMA

One evening in May 1959, the diary indicates the 21st, I was arrested for importuning. I call this a trauma. There remains some confusion as to what is a trauma. An event so emotionally powerful it leaves a scar on the psyche, something that damages our trust in others, shatters our self-image? We have moved away from an earlier definition at the time of the Great War that saw it as exposing an innate character weakness. It is said of people who are drowning that they see a flashback of their lives. On this occasion I had a flash forward, realised instantly that various futures were now ruled out, especially the rather silly idea I had of joining the Foreign Office. But trauma it was. And if trauma is also read as posing a critical choice between fight or flight, could I have reacted any differently at the time?

I was the victim of entrapment. And in fact the moment I set out after dinner from the College that May evening I was doomed. The undercover policeman who entrapped me bore a striking similarity to the PTI Royal Marine Commando whose company I had so much enjoyed on the Isle of Capri. And, indeed, as it turned out, he was a former Royal Marine. Entrapment is a barbaric practice and compounds what is already a victimless crime. Could I possibly at the time have responded with anger at this injustice? Many years later anger at this persecution is being expressed. It has done so around the case of Alan Turing. If Gordon Brown had turned down a request for the posthumous pardon of his 1952 conviction, David Cameron was to accept, Christmas Eve 2013. Chris Grayling, Justice Minister, explained: 'Dr Alan Turing was a brilliant mind.' Turing's story had already been the subject of a play, Hugh Whitmore's *Breaking the Code* and a biography by Alan Hodges. In 2011 there was a Channel 4 documentary. Hodges responded to this posthumous pardon: 'I don't think it's right in principle to make an exception for one person on the grounds of what they did for the State. It should be everyone who was in that situation.' And, in fact, notoriously some 49,000 others had been convicted under this legislation. The Pet Shop boys took up the story, performing a late night prom 23 July 2014, an ambitious piece, *A Man from the Future,* with Juliet Stephenson narrating Turing's story. Frontman Neil Tennant had already written to Cameron's office: 'could you pass on to the Prime Minister that in Alan Turing's centenary year it would be an amazing inspirational thing to pardon him.' But he was likewise averse to this being a one-off: 'we had to rewrite the ending to point out that the conviction of thousands of other men remain, and that hasn't really been discussed.' Then came the powerful film *The Imitation Game.* In its wake was An Open Letter to Her Majesty's Government, pointing out that Alan Turing was but one of 49,000 convicted: some 15,000 of these were still alive. The letter declared: 'the UK's homophobic laws made the lives of gay and bisexual men intolerable. It is up to the young leaders of today including the Duke and Duchess of Cambridge to acknowledge this mark on our history and not allow it to stand.' 'We call upon Her Majesty's Government to begin a discussion about the possibility of pardoning all the men, alive or deceased, who like Alan Turing were convicted under the UK's "gross indecency" law (Section 11 of the Criminal Law Amendment Act 1885) and under other anti-gay legislation.'

It was signed by Stephen Fry, Benedict Cumberbatch (Turing in the film), Peter Tatchell, Rachel Barnes, Turing's niece, Matthew Todd, Editor of *Attitude* magazine and N Morten Tydum, director of the film. In time a petition with over 500,000 signatures was handed over Monday 23 February to Downing Street, led by Nevil Hunt, Turing's great nephew, Rachel Barnes and her son, Thomas. Barnes said: 'I consider it to be fair and just that everybody convicted under the gross indecency law is given a pardon. It is illogical that my great uncle has been the only one to be pardoned when so many were convicted of the same crime. I feel sure that Alan Turing would have wanted justice for everybody.' Matthew Todd added: 'generations of gay and bisexual men were forced to live their lives in a state of terror.' There is rumour of a Turing law in the new parliament but I doubt if it will cover my case.

And so far, there it has rested.

Have I tried to politicise my experience? It was wholly serendipitous that the Turing case came up at the time of writing this memoir. I was aware of an earlier attempt to win pardon for offences which entailed under age sex – the law has changed from 21 to 16. But all along my only real interest is to provide a case study of how someone in the 1950s had to endure this persecution.

A former colleague at UKC told me that it was Turing's arrest that had radicalised him. But it would have taken a brave man to challenge this legislation in the 1950s, let alone one of its victims. The country was in the grip of a moral panic at homosexuality. No doubt all this was conditioned in part by the Cold War and, with the examples of Burgess and Maclean, a paranoid belief that homosexuals were peculiarly prone to treason. The Home Secretary, David Maxwell-Fyfe, had embarked on a crusade to stamp out homosexuality. (Oddly, he opposed capital punishment.) Nicholas de Jongh later wrote a play *A Plague over England,* centred on John Gielgud, one of the most celebrated victims of the crack-down. Gielgud never ceased to regret this humiliation. But I had had no excuse for not knowing the risk I ran. As a schoolboy I had followed the Montagu trial. I was so aware of danger that I even tried to alert my Father, and this would have been quite some conversation as my homosexuality was still wholly a secret, but, alas, he failed to pick up on my intention. The arrest tore down all my defences and left me horribly exposed. I chose flight. But how had I put myself in this situation? I need to look back.

In my first few days at school a boy called Crawford had touched my thigh and I got an electric shock. Public School with all its compulsory showers and changing rooms gave plenty of opportunity to satisfy my voyeurism but I still failed to make any connection here with mutual masturbation. The school scandal did make me wonder what I might have been missing and I made overtures to one of the rougher looking boys, son of a local farmer, but he was indifferent and I was but half-hearted. I was destined to leave school a virgin.

But meanwhile a truly disturbing situation had come and gone at home. I should respect the biblical injunction against shaming one's Father in the manner of Noah's sons of their drunken Father. But Father had given me, inadvertently, entirely wrong signals that he might welcome mutual masturbation. Being sexually attracted to your Father seems to be comparatively rare. Not even two such promiscuous men as Christopher Isherwood and Edmund White were. But Francis Bacon was and paid for his attraction with much welcomed sado-masochistic beatings. Father somehow steered round this appalling situation and it was never mentioned. But I wonder if an American Father would not have immediately dispatched me to a therapist. And I've no doubt, if adult sexuality is the attempt to fulfil childhood fantasy, then searching for a father figure was a huge component.

As I have already mentioned, in my view I experienced some kind of breakdown after more than three years of very intense academic work at school. I was in huge confusion over my sexuality and used to bicycle around ready for sex with just about anyone. But it did not happen. Would National Service do so? In fact the decision to go for Officer training put paid to this. In my brief spell on the lower deck I was aware of strong sexual attraction with several ordinary seamen, especially the postie on HMS

Leeds Castle. Several times a rather inebriated CPO made a pass.

My life as an Officer was wholly different. And here I think there is some cause to reflect on the nature/nurture debate. Officers were in big demand for social life in Malta and whether in naval parties or gigs at the de Trafford's home in Mdina I enjoyed a very gregarious heterosexual way of life. It was the time of rock and roll and I enjoyed dancing. There are numerous rather maudlin accounts in the journals of my enjoying female company. But do the journals indicate any physical desire?

Entries on men are very different. 6 February 1957: 'I long for the strong company of men, the frank vulgarity, the almost harsh reality.' I struck up a friendship in Venice: 'Giovanni, tall, dark, I like him but do not love him.' In the Tyrol: 'the self-assured sexuality of men. I can tolerate a sensual face but never a weak one.' There was a very strange encounter on a beach in Sliema, my equivalent to Forster's 1919 on a beach in Alexandria. A very feminine middle-aged Maltese seduced me. Not at all the person I'd have preferred and a disturbing experience.

But then came a day which set a yardstick for all future homoerotic encounters. It was on a visit to Capri, my new ship, HMS Striker on a friendly visit to Naples. Coming ashore I drifted into the company of Jim, a PTI Corporal, Royal Marine Commandos. I recorded our day together. 'By classical standards he was marred by pockmarks. But he had an outstanding virility that induced happiness. We had a fine day together looking at the Marina Piccolo and talking to the female artist at the restaurant. Then back to

Capri and to the height of Monte Salero. We seemed to have a greater ease of conversation than I'd imagined possible, mainly on sport but ranging into much talk on his own life and a little on Scotland and the arts. But he was the main conversationalist.'

But then he missed his Liberty boat. 'I put on a John Martin outfit and with the Corporal, and feeling extremely smart, I set off for a planned run ashore in this rich man's squandered Eden. For a few hours we just moved from bar to bar but eventually we discovered the number 2 Club. The Corporal considered half of them were concubines or gigolos. I found the sudden rediscovery of debauched night life intoxicating and listened to the small and excellent band with great enjoyment. At 2am we found ourselves in the top square of Capri where we drank expresso coffee in the extremely amusing company of some Canadians.'

I make no mention of our shared nudity whilst bathing, of our knees locked together in the nightclub. Alas, the Corporal on return to Malta was confined to barracks for overstepping leave. I made enquiries by phone but realised this was not a friendship I could continue under naval life at the time. But it was a memorable experience which the Eumenides were to avenge.

So by the time I reached Oxford this intolerable inexperience had to be overcome. I'm not sure anything happened in my first year. I did chat up the College gardener, an attractive former Royal Marine. The appeal lay not just in his appearance, but, as the journal puts it, in 'listening to people who have such an unquestioned acceptance of life, don't ruin it by their petty intellectual interests, or trying to understand why they have to live.' And I wrote a long piece about a Traveller I met during Christmas postal work in Radlett, William Williams, known as Squire. 'A face whose spare flesh had been creased into the lines of a familiar smile'. 'The paradox of Squire, the element of crude aggressiveness behind that smiling face, the creased smile could become a face taut and rugged remembering past struggles and future ambitions.' And indeed a difficult Cockney childhood, a drunk Father, street fighting, a vagabond existence. A good family man, children, a wife Vera: 'he liked women ugly, fat legs, thick lower lip.' He had parked his caravan by the roadside outside Borehamwood. Our odd conversations about drinking and 'a childish excitement in telling me about pissing'. He even told me of a man he caught rubbing up a horse. 'Did I ever know Squire? Did we ever break down that sense of difference into an awareness of a common humanity? Did I always remain associated with, in his words, the big uns?' I guess, though, I was already a convert to Edward Carpenter and comradeship between classes. I took rather more interest in Williams than Nicholas Richardson, also doing the Christmas post, a future brilliant historian of the Bourbon restoration.

I record in my Greek diary 1958 what I suspect was, apart from that encounter on Sliema beach, my first sexual experience, in Istanbul. I had got onto a bus and found myself pressed up against a rather plump chap I took to be Turk but in fact was Greek. Our mutual arousal soon became obvious. We arranged to meet later. This is how I describe the experience: 'I felt wooden beforehand, neither wanting nor rebelling - nagging curiosity - I sat down on the bed and tried to dissect this nebulous feeling. Did I think of Christianity, did I think of the satisfaction of desire, did I merely think it was better than any other offer? I went on the bus journey, believing it would resolve me either way. I was indifferent at being late, hoped this would resolve the conflict. But at the moment of meeting I felt silly about my doubts. But no sense of guilt. Even hearing the Iman of the Blue Mosque I was unminded of sin.' Later I met a Turkish policeman.

So sometime in my second year I took risks and had fun. Lovers would help me climb back into the college late at night. On that fatal evening I was taken to the Oxford police station, photographed and finger-printed, placed in a cell. Harry Pitt, the College Dean, came to stand bail and take me back to the College. His first question was: 'Have you always known you were homosexual?' I'm not sure how I survived the next few weeks. I'm not even sure if at first many people knew till the trial. The only overt hostility I can recall was from the College Head porter, Mr Parker.

I was in turmoil. There are long entries in the diary and these I'll have to put down verbatim.

21 May. 'Not even the shape of these words has any great meaning any longer. The feeble labyrinthine scrawl, the dry marks of my spidery being.'

'But I must try and focus on the near situation of madness. Now or never can I break the present diseased personality and travel into a new awareness of myself. O true I loathe this character, not because I believe it to be unreal but because I can see it for what it is - bourgeois, limited, undisciplined, unimaginative, a poseur, a would-be. Everything is would-be. But now I can break from it.'

'I think that at every stage we must force ourselves to the brink of madness. I must see myself in terms of the persecuted animal. I can clearly see that the individual can be tortured into imbecility by his society. He can live to be a living witness of this torture but this will only delay the process of ultimate madness, like the women keening out of excessive grief in the Karamazof Brothers. There is an escape whose major consolation is that it is self-willed - that is the deliberate courting of the finest barrier, the most exquisite of all, the self-imposed darkness of madness.'

'The most intelligent policy I can adopt is to retreat to the Warneford. It is useless my trying to pick up the strands of this unravelled being. I must rethread the wheels of the fates.'

'There is a chance for a new construction, a new essence, plumbing an unappreciated depth in this old being, something in loving sympathy with the great poets, the writers, the philosophers. How to get there when no one, not Michael, not Norman, not Andrew, will ever listen to my claims. They will postulate the convenient norm of rationality, they will stress a sincerity to myself which I must to my utmost ignore. I cannot stay as I am. Three or even more times my whole character has been challenged - once when I desired intensely to leave Gresham's, once when they threatened to take away my Commission, once when they accused me of not being worthy of my scholarship and on all occasions I accepted their criticisms. I tried to reintegrate myself with these societies. I admitted they could claim me or spew me out. I saw they could mould me and I was impotent. But these were only limited societies. Now all the forces can turn themselves against me, the police, the law, the press, my own college, my relations, all can turn their penetrating critical vision upon me and can drive me under. I shall seek the solace of self-knowledge at the expense of sanity.'

But was a new identity blocked by my 'crime'? 'It is now impossible for me even to attempt to break with the old character and attempt to express a new personality because of this new impenetrable barrier that has shut down like a portcullis.'

'I see this new barrier as totally artificial and unreal and hence will not attempt to break it down. Still, I'll not give upon a quest for a new personality though I see its quest as doomed.' 'Neurosis is inevitable and schizophrenia will be between 1) me as I am 2) me as I wish to be and 3) me as society sees me to be. All opposed.' Here was paranoia piled on paranoia.

23 May. I seem to be taking a new approach:

'the appalling escapism of my ideas. I'd refused to admit that society had any claims on me. I could choose my own strictly individual road. But this was clearly absurd. "They" had entangled me in the web of their cruel conventions. Suddenly I saw the way to surrender. I had to confess like Smith in *1984* that 2 and 2 made 5. I would have to obey the norm. The manner of expressing this obedience lay in meeting the most obvious demand of my upbringing - enter my Father's firm and become a successful bourgeois solicitor. The only possible evasion of the full dullness of the legal profession was to take an active interest in criminology and use this as a vehicle for my interest in psychology. The whole idea of surrender to what I saw as reason and common-sense was the most effective sedative to that night of mental derangement.'

Alternatively: 'I think the most difficult problem we have to face in striving for self-knowledge is overcoming our fear that what we state of ourselves is pretentiousness. In fear of insincerity we react against our uneasy because unrealised statements of our personality and seek security in more conventional types of behaviour. Only the very strong can overcome that sense of their own ridiculousness, overcome the desire for anonymity and drive themselves towards a full social or creative expression of their essential personality.' Could this be read as a readiness to 'come out' as a homosexual?

'I think there is such a thing as Providence. The entire continual thread of irony in the actual events of that night, the crowning irony was that I returned to meet the very man who arrested me and the fact that he was the nearest I had yet attained to the ideal of my Capri memory.'

'But what has suddenly hit me with a frightening sense of determinism is the nearness of my intellectual and spiritual outlook to that of Kierkegaard. His journal begins at my own age of near 22. The coincidence of this and my first reading him at this crucial moment of "either/or" must surely sway me considerably in my choice.'

A sermon by the Reverend Lee at St Mary's was, however, a warning. To quote: 'Lee was attacking those who seek in Christianity some barrier from this world in which they can establish an esoteric self-centred relationship with God. It was, he said, the path of failure.'

My attitudes to History still did not look promising: 'it becomes hideously clear that Oxford historical society verges on acute anaemia. Can I really hope to sense purpose and meaning in a grappling for factual truth? I wish to go beyond overt action into the confused web of unconscious mental processes. I am really usurping the task of the novelist. Kennan's clear-cut distinction of the tasks of the historian and novelist is one that I am loath to keep.'

But nor was I hopeful of psychiatry: 'psychiatry will neglect the wish "to become", will merely see the establishment of the equilibrium of the status quo as essential. It will determine and fix. It is for founding a character and for destroying the personality.' (I'd picked up this distinction between character and personality from Herbert Read.)

Then 27 May came the trial. Father attended. I was advised to plead guilty which I did. I received a small fine. 'Well I've now been hounded in and out of court. Surprisingly the case didn't sound so monstrous. Cannot imagine why the magistrates made no effort to discriminate my case from the others.' The policeman made up a cock and bull story. It was unnerving to see my name in the stop press of the Evening Standard.

Hoult Taylor was the only person from the past to send a letter of support: 'You will learn that you have to endure this.'

My response to the trauma was flight. So to a period of retreat in the Warneford mental hospital. The Warneford was seen as the University's extra college, with both students and dons taking advantage of its expertise. At the time of the foundation of the Radcliffe Infirmary in 1770, there had been plans for a Radcliffe Lunatic asylum. This was founded only in 27 August 1821. Several colleges gave donations and Convocation a sum from the University Chest. But the all important donation of the enormous sum of £70,000 in 1843 was from the Reverend Warneford (1763-1855), and hence its name. It was socially elitist and seen as a hospital for 'mental patients belonging to the educated classes'. 'Unselected lunatics' went to the Littlemore Asylum. There were even provisions for the separation of the better off. The sexes were strictly segregated. Once there had been compulsory prayers. It was designed 'to recreate the atmosphere of a gentleman's country club'. Indeed, set in substantial grounds, it was an attractive building. Reluctantly, it had joined the NHS after the war, otherwise its costs to 'the educated classes' would have been prohibitive.

When I entered the two key figures were Dr Scottowe and Miss May Davidson. Scottowe, a man with a large head and alarmingly strong spectacles, his eyes became enormous, was a disciple of William Sergeant. He was a fellow materialist, believed in such physical treatments as

ECT and deep insulin therapy, and was but a reluctant convert to the talking cure or psychotherapy.

Here Miss Davidson was key. She was a somewhat legendary figure. She was South African by origin where she qualified as a scientist and chemist. Then she trained in London as an educational psychologist and for a while worked under the notorious Cyril Burt. He was accused of faking evidence on some Irish school but Miss Davidson came to his rescue by asserting it was she who had collected the evidence. Quite how she became a clinical psychologist is unclear to me. I don't believe she belonged to any psychological school though out of my encounter with her I became a Freudian. But she was the ideal appointment to deal with disturbed Oxford undergraduates. I learn from a *Festshrift* for her edited by Neil Cheshire, my informant on the Warneford, that we were seen as 'May's poppets'. He adds: 'they could count upon receiving from May in generous measure that unique amalgam of psychometric diagnosis, clinical psychotherapy and academic counselling, which smaller minds sometimes could not distinguish from over indulgence'. (p.74) She was a short, dumpy woman, and a chain smoker.

Initially I was under the care of Scottowe and he subjected me to deep insulin therapy. This was for endogenous depression. This was inappropriate in my case as mine was but reactive. Later I learnt that the treatment was already seen as controversial by 1956 and was later withdrawn. Only much later did I learn this could have been life threatening. I have also wondered, unscientifically, if it triggered my later diabetes. We were put out for some four hours. On coming round we had to absorb a lot of sugar. This went on for some four weeks. We were a strange little group, just three of us. I was attracted to Bill, an ex-RAF fellow, he was attracted to Humphrey, a manic undergraduate, and Humphrey was just off the wall. What did this achieve? I put on two stone. I was lucky to be spared ECT but I was nevertheless a guinea pig in a merely experimental treatment and this is almost criminal.

And then I was transferred to Miss Davidson. I took a whole battery of psychological tests. I was fascinated by the Rorschach test and knew that how I responded to the red dots was critical. Miss Davidson had met some of the family earlier on, but she only ever mentioned my Mother. One of the first things she ever said to me, 'your Mother is a very silly woman.' Did she believe she had to overcome a Mother fixation? In a way my whole life had been building up for a psychotherapeutic encounter. I was a natural candidate. She was honest with me. The aim was to fit me, a round peg into a square hole. I was to be groomed as a conformist. Her technique was the dynamic of silence. She might place a question and then wait. More often she left it to me to take the initiative. Long silences, with her chain smoking. But I tended to break first. But she was trying to change me. She wanted to bring me down to earth and have a more realistic attitude to life. Here was a battle over my personal integrity. She also believed she could 'turn' me into a heterosexual. I recall our talking about Marilyn Monroe and her saying that the heterosexual act was very simple. In retrospect it is unfortunate she did not encourage me to accept myself as homosexual, but then this was the 1950s and it remained anathema. Would I learn to come into line with social reality?

I wrote little on the early days. The first entry is for 20 June. 'It was odd how my attitude to the Warneford changed. I looked on it first as the most comforting of retreats. Then, when I saw it as a place for a long time stay, I grew afraid of it. This was my customary fear of obeying a system. But I've gradually worn this fear away.'

'It is a double life I will lead here: on the one hand, a solitary reflective life, on the other, the negation of my essential self in touching on the personalities of all the other inmates.'

'I've fought shy of introspection since the trial. The greatest struggle was winning back some kind of recognition by society. I think I probably over-tested myself. The task was in fact easier than I had anticipated. But the effort was deleterious. I fought very hard against coming to the Warneford. But I've come to perceive the obvious value of my being here.' (First mention of my resisting coming to the Warneford?)

One evening on a long walk beyond the hospital grounds, 'I saw why I had come to the Warneford. It wasn't because of any minor depressed state following the trial. It was for the reason that my whole way of thinking was leading me away from society, from physical happiness, into a hideous isolation. Quite clearly I cannot hope to tackle a year of grinding study until I have formulated some more coherent pattern of life for myself.'

'I walked round the grounds and allowed the sense of isolation to expand into the wholeness of the universe. There is a very persistent awareness of the universal here. At evening I know I live at the centre of the symbolic world of earth, sky, moon and sun. Even the tree, the furrow, the mauve evening light are meaningful as universal. But I also recognise my own appalling inadequacy before this spacious universality. I try to fill the space with my personality, try and grasp and give some definite verbal expression to the sense of the universal. But I can only wish for this spaciousness to crumble and disintegrate into the tormented figure of a Romanesque Christ in a fractured sky. I resent the roundness of the circular. Maybe I resent the feminine. I demand the jagged, the broken, the angular features of the masculine.' (Odd premonitions here of Mishima's novels.)

Then another long gap, 25th July. 'I fear the stay at the Warneford was essential. I had it within me to behave with extreme irresponsibility, suicide, spiting my own face to revenge myself on others through remorse.'

'It was a time of furious introspection balanced by moments of self-ridicule and stretches of inertia.'

'I should like to think the moods of self-enquiry were valuable. I think I was plunging ahead of myself. And I have probably foretold a manner of life I may not be able to sustain for several decades to come. One leading theme was the possibility of a genius for prayer. If one lacks the capacity for expressing ideas in a permanent art-form, it might well be that one can dedicate the pure thought in prayer to God. The danger of mysticism as such is the destruction of individuality. But this fear I reject.'

More on History. 'It would be wrong to argue that the study of modern history is really the study of the prolonged death-throws of mankind. I think the incredible confusion we are faced with today is the inevitable price of knowledge. The conflict of good and evil becomes huger in ratio to the increase of knowledge. The truly strong man is he who can bring himself to the very edge of indecision, yet ignore the experience of evil for the sake of its understanding (Is this a rejection of Dostoyevsky?) and still choose the good. If I can deny myself experience I could assume a spiritual way of life. But at the moment I am lost in the body, in the sharp conflict of mind and body.'

'The intellectual is one who can grasp an idea and act upon it. I am not an intellectual because I follow the dictates of the body in complete contradiction to the understanding of the mind.'

I am not sure at what point I transferred to Ward 5, Oxford's alternative undergraduate college. But I think it was still in the main hospital that I was to be so distressed at an apparent racist slur on a Nigerian undergraduate on whom I had a crush. The staff had to rescue me from the grounds in a state of emotional collapse. Probably this set me on the path of anti-racism all my life. Years later we met again in Lagos but he was incurably heterosexual. There was a disturbing moment finding myself in the same bathroom as another patient, lolling in the bath, who was undergoing gender reassignment. S/he was attracted to me. S/he worked for OUP and I still own the Atlas s/he gave me. In Ward 5 I got to know other undergraduates. One was a Scholar from Corpus, struggling to come to terms with being the middle of three brothers. Miss Davidson had to warn me off from any friendship with a highly vulnerable schizophrenic girl, clearly attracted to me. Being absorbed into this hospital community took up most of my energies over the long vacation. Arguably, all this was the most formative experience of my undergraduate years.

By September I could write in the diary: 'And so it was not really a question of Either/Or at all. It is simply a problem of development. Dear Miss D - she has seen through my fogginess all the time. And I thought I was talking myself into emptiness. My only fear is that the present clarity will follow the usual career - it entails no action - soon the extra acquisition of knowledge leads to further confusion - and not even the barbed moon can free me from that entanglement.'

21 September

'Just think what a force it would be if an introvert were suddenly to release his dammed up feelings in spontaneous extravert behaviour. If the full force of his personality were to be boldly projected at society. How shallow people are who clearly do present their personalities in a habitual extravert manner: they should bowl over their friends by their vitality. No-one who fails to stagger his friends by his total personality can be of any value-they are ghosts, not people.'

24 September

'It may be that I have a vocation for suffering. It may be that the conspiracy by society contains the answer to the problem of vocation. Of course this has been done before - Verlaine, Rimbaud. But it may simply be a question of discovering myself through suffering, not for the sake of self-understanding, but merely so that others can see how such a person does undergo the stress of suffering. I accept the position of guinea-pig. There are people who are not big enough to realise their own tragedy.'

I left the Warneford to take up the third year. The College had decided against an aegrotat intermission. However, I continued to see Miss Davidson throughout this year. Undergraduates normally produce their best work in their third year and this raises the possibility of a First. I, in fact, produced some of my weakest work and Harry Pitt later recognised that I was held back by personal problems. Yet I was to be rescued. I was awarded a Senior Scholarship to St Antony's College. I was to be given a second chance.

So what were the negatives and positives from managing the trauma?

I lost my Commission. I had recently been promoted to Sub-Lieutenant. In some ways I was relieved as I rather dreaded any future refresher courses in the Naval Reserve. Of course the days when gays could join the armed forces were years away. Lord Justice Simon Brown phoned me the night before making his judgement, just checking if T E Lawrence was a good example to cite of a gay in the army. In fact it was not. Lawrence may have identified with outcast illegitimate boys and sought masochistic punishment following his humiliation at Deraa, but he was not gay. Rather he was an ascetic and celibate. A better choice might have been Kitchener or Montgomery, though nothing has ever been proven of the former; and the latter, a fierce homophobe, was more a lover of adolescent boys. Maybe the war poets, Siegfried Sassoon and Wilfrid Owen, would have been best.

There were unforeseen consequences over visas for the USA. I was invited to be a Visiting Professor at the University of South Carolina, 1965-66, but no one had anticipated the problem of a visa. I endured one of the creepiest moments of my life being interviewed by a stooge gay at the American Embassy. I had naively thought if I could show I was in a stable relationship they would not worry. The visa application was refused on grounds that I was a criminal psychopath. Later, in the1980s, on a journey to Mexico, I found myself in transit at Fort William airport and confronted by a turn-style which would check whether I had visa clearance. I had been assured by the travel company that no visa for America was necessary. What to do? I guess if I had admitted to my former visa ban I might have been let through, but I risked it, and was immediately caught. I was charged with being an illegal immigrant, hand-cuffed and frog-marched onto the next plane back to Heathrow. There the Passport official moaned, ‘oh no not another one’. The Americans frequently deport visitors in breach of their visa status. So I had to get a new passport to visit Canada for a conference in Toronto a few weeks later.

But the conviction had no negative consequences for my academic career. On the contrary, I suspect St Antony's would not have elected me had the Fellows not been so outraged at the persecution of homosexuals. In 1963 I was appointed to Universities in Jamaica and Malaysia, neither country gay-friendly, though in fact I chose UCNW Bangor instead. Professor Mowat and my colleagues were charming and always very discreet. It was never mentioned.

Positively, I was drawn far more perceptively into a form of self-analysis that I had been pursuing for some time and one that I was to follow up with a major reading of Freud and the Post-Freudians. I think the book that influenced me the most was Philip Rieff's *The Mind of the Moralist*, on how to weaken the superego. Freud's metapsychology became the dominant framework for reading my life.

But there was to be a shift in values. At one moment in my sessions with Miss Davidson I mentioned I was about to read William James's *Types of Religious Experience.* She strongly discouraged me. I'm not sure why - it is steeped in a kind of American pragmatism. But I can sort of see this was to be a turning point away from religion at this stage of my life. Even so, I was in fact to make my first visit to Nashdom Abbey in, I think, January 1960 and was to work through a lot of ideas with George Silver, then Father Gregory in the monastery. But I find in the diary this rather dismissive statement: 'the hospital and the monastery are totalitarian states in miniature. But they lose their validity the moment they propagandise their faiths.' I also write: 'I recognise the validity of Christian actions and attitudes but do not commit myself to Christianity because I am not really concerned with God.' The wonderful Abbot Morris, I think in an address and not in any personal conversation, 'rejected the notion of treating God as sense experience as impossible. He cannot be treated experimentally as a chemist would sodium chloride.'

Oddly, I have no recollection of discussing with Miss Davidson my identity as a poet. But, again, I suspect this was the time when that identity lessened. And, indeed, if I were to describe the deepest way in which that process of moulding me into society worked, it was the conversion in time from a sense of myself as a poet to an acceptance of myself as a historian. Still, I wrote poetry for at least another year.

How did all this impact on my relating to family and friends?

Both my parents refused to believe that they had given birth to a homosexual. Both were convinced I had been corrupted. Father asked me by whom and I said Yorith the gardener. This was completely false and a warning to distrust what people say about childhood experience. Mother thought the reason for my seeking out men was simply because I could not afford to take out girls. She had once said that the worst thing that could befall a mother was her son turning out to be a pansy. I fear all this forfeited my treating her as a confidante in the way Isherwood did his very snobbish Mother. Father was in no way judgmental and he admitted recalling shortly before the crisis my trying to tell him my concerns. But even so, his first move was to be reassured it would not jeopardise my future legal career.

Grandfather Copley had died when I was in Malta. Granny Copley predeceased him. I rather kept my distance from all my relatives for several years. Uncle Jack, a rampant heterosexual, I could never bring myself to visit, though he lived nearby in Kent.

And I lost touch with many friends. It was a year when Michael's loyalty was very important. We shared digs in the Woodstock Road.

And what of my sexuality? Miss Davidson encouraged me to befriend girls and I was to do so. One friendship led to a wonderful stay on Loch Linnhe. Another girl from St Hilda's got very close and I'd fondle her breasts in my room in St Antony's. But we parted. My first gay affair was during my time at the Warneford. I was also exploring a friendship with Juanita from Greece days, to become my most important woman friend. She is a brilliant artist and very exciting company. But I think Foucault has got it right, writing in terms of homosexual acts rather than being gay. Once you have experienced physical pleasure from such acts, why change?

But the conviction had imposed a criminal homosexual identity on me. I now identified with all oppressed peoples, minorities, outsiders. Whether I was up till then an insider is questionable, but I was seen as such. I now felt myself to be marginalised. There had indeed been a considerable reorientation. But I believe I became a nicer person through being on the outside.

10
GRADUATE AND BEYOND: ST ANTONY'S COLLEGE 1960-63

So I was to begin all over again at St Antony's College. Here I was to resolve the adolescent crisis of identity and move into an academic career. It was the ideal college for studying modern European history in the B.Phil programme. There was to be a second visit to Greece in the summer before. I also attended the University for Foreigners in Perugia to add Italian to French: the B.Phil required a working knowledge of two European languages. I still wrote poetry in that summer but then academic study took over. Religious questions were in abeyance but this was a time when I made a long stay at Nashdom Abbey. A conflict remained between a career as a historian and the appeal of being a psychotherapist.

Juanita had invited me to Greece with the promise of some idyllic farmstead in Samos. I must have picked up a boat for Piraeus from Venice. The journal records 19th July 1960: 'daytime spent in our slothful journey through the Corinth canal. At evening the land slid towards the uterine canal and we were caught spectators of the faltering sun, whose bigness filled the exit to the sea behind. The fatness of the sun pouring from its sides like too long-satisfied flesh. It was trod into the sea as if by some God. Yet Apollo showed through. The warmth of the sun drew out the withdrawn looseness of the rock, a kind of languorous seduction.'

I took the measure of Athens. 'It is a matchbox city. Extraordinary how you can move from a soulless centre of the city into the sprawling suburbs - something helplessly half-finished about it all. The inspiration was weak, the will non-existent, seed on barren ground. Could it be a terrible failure of a primitive society to mimic the consolidated ugliness of more prosperous societies?' The suburbs were of course the result of mass Greek emigration from the Turkish mainland following the defeat of 1921 and this no doubt explains its apparent rootlessness.

It was summer of island hopping: Mykonos, Samos, Patmos. In Patmos I enjoyed some memorable religious experience. We witnessed a festival. 'The procession of the icon. Sweat falling like candle grease from the faces of the monks. The abbot blinking. They swayed beneath our house then sinuated around the town. Just like those paintings of medieval processions. The houses were empty for all had joined the procession. Even the old crone in our house had her incense burner. It occurred to me that Greece by growing more primitive relative to the rest of Europe will end by preserving a relatively more vivid religious life and this will induce her to argue self-complacently that she is the nobler race. The paradox of regression. On the other hand if the Greeks ever realised the extent to which the Church had fooled them, *quelle vengeance*!'

I went on to stay in the Monastery. I visited the cave where John the Divine had his vision. 'Into something like grotto dampness. Here St John used to wet the stones with his tears. An old man, who lay his head in a hole in the rocks and lifted himself up by a niche in the rock-face. How did the vision come? Maybe in the twilight of sleep, the dreams of heaven murky in his brain. Then the earthquake and the livid stroke of destruction down the cave roof, strangulated into the symbol of the Trinity. The murky dreams now sharply figured, a vision, the steadiness of the eagle's gaze into the blinding light of the Apocalypse. Many days after this, John, in animated relating of his vision to the deacon, Proclus.'

I was reading Freud's *Interpretation of Dreams* at the time and the journal is full of my own dreams.

So to Perugia. My stay there memorable for two friendships. One was an Indian poet, Ronnie Banerjee. I never discovered his precise origins (Bengali) but Indian-educated before taking a degree at Edinburgh under Richard Pares. He was in conflict with a girlfriend, Gale - she had been unfaithful - and there was a choice between her love and the inspiration it brought and his holding out for his moral integrity without her. I was myself reading Nietzsche at the time and drawn to the aphorism.

Here are some of Ronnie's.

'Distrust the female: too treacherous to allow access to his intellectual schema.'

'I prefer to believe in certain myths at the expense of philosophical truths. But I am sincere in my emotions.'

'I find I have to make a choice between being truthful and between being a worthless fellow, yet an artist.'

'I am indifferent to the picture of myself I present to others.'

Yet his poetry was a disappointment, fine sentiment, disciplined craftsmanship, but lacking all contemporaneity. 'The particular was sunk in a big language. The feelings were aristocratic. But the language itself was uneven. He could not always stretch to the big word. The banal and the fine must always be contrasted deliberately.'

Hannes was an Afrikaaner and I was surprisingly tolerant in listening to his apologia for apartheid: 'in his slow gawkish way he got across a real defence. Extraordinary how sex crept in. His definite view of the blacks as incurably dirty. I don't see why I should have them clinging on my neck for the next two hundred years. Unwilling to take on the role of "civiliser". The argument that South African apartheid stems from a historical situation intrinsically different from other histories of black and white races. Elsewhere the races were never closely integrated and could separate easily. In South Africa by a slow historical process the races became intertwined. The process of separation must be harsher. The interesting economic claim. We will build up a cheap white labour market. Hordes of Italians ready to migrate to South Africa. There will be no problems of the races living together in slum districts.' (Was I just a little sexually attracted to him? And of course all this was dangerous special pleading.)

They both thought I had to be a Catholic after giving a synopsis of Cathar doctrine.

Bannerjee told me to write. 'The first novel would serve the function of self-elucidation. The test is to force oneself into the myth that one has something important to say.'

Ronnie's statement: 'I don't see you as Jupiterish, the serene scholar. I see you as more impulsive, a fusion of Mercury and Saturn.'

There is this entry. 'I am convinced I saw death. At first I believed him to be a policeman. Stood in the rain, hooded, something Austrian and dated about his clothes. Spying me out in the degenerate track of my sin. But he had gone the next time I passed. But now, reading a book, I suddenly started with recognition. I stared into a mirror at an angle. But I did not appear. This was a vision of death. This no ordinary fear. A sudden sense of completion. The parting of the fake from the real and the trudge to destiny.'

'Jung and the libido - he sees it as a primordial sub-consciousness, potently urging archetypal visions into the personality. Freud limited it to the sex drive, distinguishing it from ego instincts.' Many reflections in my journal on psychology.

All kinds of floundering views on what kind of history I should study. 'I am interested in mediaeval history as a historian. I am only interested in modern history as a tuning fork for the rhythm of creation and destruction in the modern world. You can combine mediaeval scholarship with a completely emotional drive towards the modern world. This is the best combination.'

'Modern history has more material. I can more readily turn to biography, probably my strongest interest. Also the literature and philosophy are more important. I think the crucial figure in modern history is the apocalyptic politician.' So I was slowly moving towards accepting myself as a modernist.

And I was having to wrestle with the question of whether still to visit Miss Davidson. 'I recognise now that I have got a good insight into myself but with a violent swing of mood I again lose control. I see her as a guide who is certainly leading the personality in the right way but is taking over my will. It as if I still have another father-mother symbol without really discovering a truly subjective will.' I cut loose.

St Antony's was very new, opened in 1958. At short notice the University authorities had to find a building to present to the shipping magnate, M. Besse, who announced he was coming to see the college he had founded with a donation of a million pounds. A convent belonging to the nuns of St Antony of Padua had just come on the market and it was purchased. I assume the College Warden and fellows had already been appointed. In fact I'd lived in digs in my third undergraduate year in the Woodstock Road right opposite the college. This was to be but a short move.

My tutor was James Joll, everyone agrees the nicest man around, and the most cultured man to teach me; but we were far too shy to get to know each other well. My Scholarship was remarkably permissive and I could do whatever I liked with it. I even thought of an undergraduate degree in Theology. Initially I'd thought of a B.Phil in Politics and visited Max Beloff in All Souls to discuss the possibility. I was a natural at political theory. When I returned later to come to a decision he claimed not to know me and announced there were days when he did not even recognise his family. That put paid to that idea. St Antony's had not yet taken on the complexion of a set of regional centres in Europe, the Middle East, Latin America, Japan etc. It had a wonderfully open-ended recruitment, philosophers, chemists, if mainly those in history and politics, several from active service, the Sudanese civil service, the American State department. It was however ideal for the study of modern European history. In my interview I'd seen myself as a Risorgimento historian in the making, so excited had I been by my journeys in Sicily and the toe of Italy. But in the end I went for Church and State in France and this was a good choice. It raised religious and moral questions that occupied my life. Probably in this still fluid period the College had never been so intellectually stimulating.

The College had a reputation as a college for spies. James had been in intelligence during the war. David Footman, a Russian specialist, had been a spy. Russian studies were very strong, with the old fashioned monarchist, Katkov and the brilliant translator, Max Hayward as Fellows. The Warden, Bill Deakin, possibly the most charming man I have ever met, had been active in SOE in Yugoslavia. He arranged a superb seminar on all of this in my time there, graced by the leonine figure of Vladimir Dedijer. I was rather disillusioned later to discover how closely the College had worked with the CIA. But the internal politics of the college at the time seems to have passed me by. There were furious debates over the admission of women. I do recall sharing intense collegiate anxiety during the Cuban Missile crisis.

It is silly to think of myself at St Antony's as an outsider. Its Senior Scholarships, after the All Souls Fellowships by examination, were possibly the most sought out graduate awards at Oxford. Mine was a particularly talented entry. There was cultural historian to be, Peter Burke. A close friend as an undergraduate, and a little surprisingly I was to be his Best Man, was Henry Kamen, historian of early modern Spain. I was very taken by Peter Cairns, Winchester and New, a Russian coder and embarked on a doctoral project on Bukharin. At his viva it became clear he had not read many of his special subject texts, so he only got a 2nd. Tragically, and before a cure had been found, he was later diagnosed with Hodgkin's disease, and he decided just to enjoy what was left of his life, qualified in insurance, and lived out his remaining days in gay New York. He almost persuaded me to take a serious interest in jazz. In my year was also the beguiling Polish philosopher, Henryk Scolomowski, Miklos Veto, a Hungarian refugee from 1956, a philosopher, and the patriarchal Croat, our JCR President, Chris Cviic. Neal Blewett and John Roberts both had future political careers. In my second year Brian Harrison and philosopher Tim Moore joined. Julian Mitchell also joined that year and was to cause mayhem in the sexual tensions of the college.

Highly talented Tim Mason came in my third year. I failed to read his bi-polar condition and his later suicide in Rome was a great shock. Together we won the College tennis doubles in 1963. It was at St Antony's that my very close friendship with Rod Kedward finally matured. But the most exciting of my friendships at the time was with Martin Gilbert.

I had already admired Martin as an undergraduate. By chance we found ourselves in adjacent rooms in one of the college's houses in Winchester Road. I was very flattered to become his friend. Maybe I served the same role for Martin as Julian Ayers had done at Magdalen, a kind of confidante. At one level I saw it as an acting out of Hannah Arendt's theory in the *Origins of Totalitarianism* that the fate of the Jews and of homosexuals were ineluctably linked in the 20th century, the key connecting figure, Marcel Proust. For all his academic brilliance Martin was often crippled by the demands of his personal life. On 15 November 1960 the journal records: 'I told Michael (Williams) in a letter that friendships had lost their tangibility. Yet I'm exposed to the full flood of Martin Gilbert's emotional troubles. He told me he'd broken down in tears when Maureen (Rosenthal) came and told him she no longer cared for him as in the old way.' It was a role I took on all over again when his second marriage with Susie was breaking down. He had been evicted from the family home and I stayed with him in his flat in St John's Wood. He was also recovering from a multiple by-pass operation. Susie had insisted he consult a psychiatrist, convinced, as she was, that it was all a form of madness and that he would come to his senses. Martin and I chuckled over the psychiatrist's theory that all his problems with women stemmed from resentment at his Mother sending him to Canada during the war as a refugee. In fact Martin's third marriage to Esther finally brought him real domestic happiness. I was taken aback when I first met her - she seemed so alike in appearance to Susie - but she was a far calmer and more compliant person.

Martin was a genius at planning travel and I was lucky in this first year at St Antony's to enjoy two holidays together. In a letter 2 December 1973, reflecting on our visit to Paris, he wrote: 'it is still my favourite city for being totally removed from daily problems and pressure of work: and it seems to accept so readily the quest for anonymity. I wonder where Frenchmen find that same escape.' We walked ourselves into exhaustion and only survived through consuming those wonderful French patisseries. Martin recalled in a letter 23 October 1997: 'I keep remembering our Paris time together. Like you I suspect that the cream cakes would prove far too risky for today. I am actually on a ferocious diet just now and have lost eight pounds in ten days.' It was in our shared bedroom in Paris that I made a very rare confession to Martin of my homosexuality and my criminal conviction, all of which he took in a very matter of fact sort of way. Yet in letter to Juanita there is this strange admission: 'my sorry return from Paris - mounting tension between Martin and I, our friendship never an easy one, lost I suspect permanently whatever equilibrium it possessed'. Of course, our friendship remained intact and was to be a lifetime friendship. But a possible explanation for this anxiety lies in this observation in a letter from Martin, 28 February

1979, all about India and I'll quote it later more fully: 'the world seems a more wicked place somehow than when we walked in the streets in Paris, arguing about whether Nazi criminals should hang after fifteen years had elapsed since the end of the war. Do you remember that? Yours was the voice of persuasive morality.' We had clearly differed over their fate but who had supported execution, who clemency?

On another occasion we journeyed to Frankfurt, hired a car to travel to Vienna and back, via Italy. Did we visit Venice? Somewhere Martin misread the right of way and we collided with a car as we crossed the dual carriageway. Fortunately neither passenger nor car was badly hurt. In the crypt of St Florian's, confronted by a pile of skulls, Martin and I both had a fit of the giggles. In Vienna we just turned up at the Opera house and got tickets for *Cosi fan Tutte*, sung by Elizabeth Schwarzkopf and Victoria de los Angeles.

A later holiday to Israel in 1981 was not so successful. I was invited to join the Sacker family to witness the bar mitzvah of Susie's younger brother. It was held dramatically at Masada, taken by the likeable Rabbi Hugo Gryn. But I was staying in Susie's parents flat and overstayed my welcome. I was dined in Mandy Rice Davies's Chinese restaurant, and Martin took me on a journey past the scene of the Good Samaritan to Jericho. I attended surely the longest seminar Martin ever gave at the University of Tel Aviv on the Balfour declaration: all of 8 hours. I also met a number of Jerusalem academics. They struck me as seeing themselves as provincial, the real world being in London and New York. I fortunately met a local psychiatrist and he looked after me. I was more sympathetic to Judaism than Christianity at the time and though I saw many of the main Christian sites I took the chance to stay in the Jewish mystical centre of Safad. Some weeks after my return I fell down with hepatitis A. I was told it was probably contracted from infected sea food. I passionately shared Martin's engagement with the Holocaust but grew more distant from his Zionism.

As an undergraduate Martin had hitch-hiked to India across Turkey, Iran and Afghanistan, arriving more dead than alive. In Bombay he had been restored to health by the parents of his friend Prem Jha at Magdalen, Auntie Fori, as he came to call her, and her diplomatic husband, B K Nehru. It inspired a love affair for India and at St Antony's he was registered to do a doctorate on Indian famines. But this was to be replaced by the Churchill project. One of the most remarkable letters he wrote, 28 February 1975, marked a change. Already in a post-card he sent me at Ibadan from India, 4 November 1974, he wrote: 'Bombay, Ahmedabad, and now Benares have quite cured me of romantic India.' He continues: 'famine in the west, filth and poverty here, apathy overall - I've had enough.' In the letter he expressed horror at Jawaharlal Nehru's looking on the plight of the Harijans as a mere side-show: 'I believe that the rights of 60 million people cannot be dismissed or daily lives made so grim.' Then he saw people dying from famine: 'Mrs Gandhi announced there was no famine. Such hypocrisy sickens me. Why should I hide such feelings to you. They have nothing to do with my life-long feelings of sympathy towards India and the

Indians: a sympathy which my visit last year served to **strengthen**.' His ethical code was outraged, 'admittedly narrowly Judaeo-Christian, but one central measure of civilised behaviour, both of States and individuals, is the attitude to the sufferings of each man, whatever his birthmark, or "colour". You were among the few people who helped to inculcate those values in me: so don't be annoyed when I seek to retain them not only in the face of Indian philosophy but in the face of many daily breaches all over the world. Torture of prisoners, arrest without trial, censorship of fair comment, neglect of minorities, police tyranny: all that I hate, and was **deeply** shaken to find so many of them practised in India. Some of my Indian friends were themselves much more pessimistic about the manifestations than they had been even two years before. (A reference to Mrs Gandhi's Emergency regime.) Perhaps it will change again. History charts an erratic course for mankind. But just now I felt India a grim place for human dignity. I got no pleasure from the degradations I saw: yes it was a bad year as you say.' Martin kept in touch with India out of his love for Aunti Fori. He discovered she was in fact a Hungarian Jew, and, to enlighten her on her faith, he wrote his delightful *Letters to Auntie Fori.* I rather suspect it was his air travel to India in December 2011 that put a strain on his heart and accounts for his collapse in Jerusalem in March 2012.

We could not have been more different as historians. He had a real genius for marshalling evidence. But there was a twist. As the Times's obituarist put it: 'no other historian has adhered so rigidly to the facts and so adamantly refused to speculate or theorise or impose preconceived notions on the available evidence.' You would not turn to Martin for interpretation. He saw himself as a chronicler. I wonder though if that is quite compatible with an insistence on being absolutely confident in what you write. He would always avoid 'perhaps'. 'It is for the historian either to say what happened or to say that he cannot discover it. To say "perhaps it was like this" is to mask a failure to get to the bottom of the problem.' In marked contrast, I was always ready to write in terms of the ambiguity of events and one book I wrote, *Sexual Moralities in France 1780-1980* was notorious for its frequent use of 'perhaps'. Yet maybe it was Martin who subtly won me over to being a historian in that first year at St Antony's when he suggested that being a historian is rather like being a psychoanalyst of the past, searching for the truth.

To celebrate his 78th birthday, Martin hired the very boat that carried Churchill's coffin up river. Family and friends joined the boat at Katherine's dock and we chugged down river to the barrier and back up to Westminster, all the while being provided delicious food. I'd never seen the river at night, all lit up. It was memorable evening. It is just too sad to write of his last years, though Esther made a heroic effort to make these as comfortable as possible. The last time I saw him was after Gordon Brown had formally opened the Sir Martin Gilbert library at Highgate School.

An interesting College visit, by way of return of hospitality, was to the Free University of West Berlin, June 1961. I was never to go to Berlin with the Wall. I wrote of the city, 'growing out of a historical vacuum, the soullessness of the city'. In a letter to Juanita, saying how useless Isherwood was now as a guide, 'Berlin is now a highly complex city in a political sense, but which hides it all behind a provincial face, where the insistence on material ordinariness, or stoical common-sense has killed the élan and cosmopolitanism of a great city.' In fact, I recall West Berlin as a brilliant show case for western capitalism, with the glamour of its modernist high rise architecture, its hedonistic life-style. The city seemed far more dowdy when I returned in the 1990s.

Two students at the Free University stand out. One a frightening young man of extreme patriotic views, with cruel but clear observations on Germany's immediate past, determined on reunification, and I forecast a tricky customer in whatever future field he turned up in. He taunted me to swim out into the middle of Lake Wannsee and I, a poor swimmer, was very relieved to make it back to the shore. But the other student I rather fell for. 'Older than the rest, diffident and hedged in at some level, casual slouched physique with rather an ugly face. He somehow came to represent everything that was typical of the present generation of West Berlin. He grew up under the blitz and watched his city develop its contemporary political schizophrenia, and himself acquire the same neurotic outlook of this metaphorically diseased city. His old home had been in the former administrative area of the city, now in communist hands, all flattened by the blitz. Prematurely he had taken over the running of his Father's school, on the verge of bankruptcy, just as the city had taken on the task of reconstruction. And just as the city had only half-triumphed, now divided with an anxious population, so he in fact survived with a now thriving school, but with an internal block, a sense of himself as a private failure, no real grasp of life.' We had met before on his visit to St Antony's. 'I was astonished at the possibilities of communication with a foreigner, suddenly recognising the similarity of people, all puzzling over like problems, if in seemingly very different environments.' But I never conveyed to him his sexual attractiveness.

My next foreign stay was in Paris to research my thesis for the B.Phil. It's a measure of how far we were left to our own devices that I struck on the very esoteric subject of the setting up of Free Catholic universities in the 1870s. Still, it meant I became very well informed on Catholic thought and this proved invaluable in the examination. One of my examiners, Agnes Headlam-Morley was a devout catholic and was no doubt very impressed. Rod had alighted on a similarly marginal topic of the attempted *coup* of the Duc de Broglie in the same decade. It was in Paris that we became much closer. I shall never forget his kindness on my first night of taking over my tripe which I had mistakenly ordered at our cafeteria. I hate tripe. Poulenc always saw promiscuity as the royal road to affairs and I was very lucky in meeting Franco-Italian Angelo, a successful plasterer, in Pigalle, and enjoyed my visits to his flat. It was a love affair renewed in 1979 when I was researching French attitudes to divorce and homosexuality.

I was far from confident I'd done well enough in the B.Phil examination. I'd retreated in my anxiety to the Warneford and it was Miss Davidson who phoned Schools to see if my name was on the pass list. Later, my supervisor for Church and State and one of my examiners, Wilfrid

Knapp, wrote: 'I was very happy about your B.Phil result. I had inevitably been worried about the position I should find myself in, judging as your tutor that you should reach the standard required without too much difficulty, anxious that as your examiner I might have to be excessively critical. In the event there was no difficulty. Your papers in Church and State were very good, the thesis potentially good but needing some extra work to pull it together. The most important thing was that all your papers gave evidence of distinction. In a way it is easy to mark the B.Phil because one looks out for this particular quality and neither Agnes nor I had any doubt we saw it in your work. The reason why your European history was not so good was that we obviously did not set the right questions.' And, indeed, I had struggled. The longest essay I wrote for James Joll was on Freud and the post-Freudians and not a hint of this in the examination. Harry Pitt wrote: 'I'm delighted to see your B.Phil result. My warm congratulations. It's nice for Worcester too.' Beryl Smalley, my much loved tutor of St Bernard, wrote: 'Congratulations on the B.Phil which I hear was a "good one" (and even the bad ones are pretty difficult to get.) and I hope you'll find something interesting to do with it.' And, of course, that was the big question. I'm glad to say the degree was upgraded to M.Phil. Myself and my family had been rather humiliated in Senate House when hordes of MA's preceded us humble B.Phils.

I still had a year to run of my Senior Scholarship. I registered for a Ph.D under Theodore Zeldin on Jules Simon. I compiled a substantial bibliography but there it rested. Later though I chose a like liberal conservative figure in the Indian National Congress, Rajagopalachari, an admirer of Edmund Burke and J S Mill, and pursued this project to a conclusion, with the publication of *The Political Career of C Rajagopalachari 1937-54* (Macmillan 1978). Meanwhile at Oxford I turned my attention to Spain, attended Raymond Carr's lucid and brilliantly structured lectures on Modern Spain and wrote a paper on The Spanish Left in the 1930s for David Caute's seminar on the Left and the Right in 20th century Europe.

Yet I was still unsure what career to pursue. Should I be a psychotherapist or an academic historian? Miss Davidson insisted I'd have to have a desire to heal to be a therapist and I believed, according to my definition, this was so, helping others to acquire an insight into themselves. So, thoughts such as these in the journal: 'I see psychology as the study of essential man, the naked man: it is a highly philosophical and religious discipline and the great contemporary science.' 'I feel convinced I would be an excellent psychotherapist.' 'Is it not a matter of emotional involvement? Clearly I'm far more disturbed by psychology. Its subject matter confuses me far more totally than history. Such emotional activity is a necessary precondition for any real intellectual achievement. The challenge lies in the capacity for pitting detachment against such emotion.' But against: 'it would be a withdrawn career. The constant contact with the mentally ill might prove too great a strain.' The idea of measuring endless psychological tests did not appeal. And I think it was Miss Davidson's probing that produced this insight: 'it maybe that the pleasure gained from the fantasy of being a psychotherapist is out of a purely negative rejection of society. The non-moralising role of the psychologist is a deliberate rejection of a moralising society.' And at a deeper level: 'I cannot decide between intellectual order or experience, between discipline and some scholastic structure or the old self-annihilating life, the experiential.'

Did I ever see being a historian as a vocation? Midway in preparing for the B.Phil I wrote: 'But I do not deny that the role of a lecturer in a complex society has appeal. Maybe not Oxford. But Africa? Asia? Somehow there is still an existential identification to make. Though I doubt if I have really estimated the hugeness of the choice.'

Later: 'yet few subjects are of such lasting interest as history even if I am quite incapable of identifying myself with the name Historian.'

So with the B.Phil behind me, was it becoming clearer? 'I've no doubt that I would be a conscientious and rewarding teacher. I'm genuinely concerned at emancipating minds. Providing I can escape the temptation of seeing them as sick. And clearly the opportunities for helping people and the need for psychological insight are demands in any teaching career.' I was now thinking in terms of the post-Robbins new universities. Maybe I had discovered a vocation, to teach.

At one stage I began to wonder if life outside Oxford was possible and tried for a research fellowship by examination at Magdalen. But I had to make a choice. In the end I applied for three universities, UCNW Bangor; Kingston, Jamaica; Kuala Lumpur, Malaysia. I was offered all three. But Oxford academics recommended caution. I might never return from overseas. I could always teach abroad later on. So I made a conservative and pragmatic choice and accepted Bangor.

I've no wish to pursue a narrative of my career beyond this point. I enjoyed three and half very happy years at Bangor and often dreamt of returning. I was haunted by the beauty of the view from Beaumaris, where I stayed all my time there, of the Menai Straits and Snowdonia. Probably at no stage of my career was I so looked up to by students, and I believe the lectures I gave on Modern Europe and my Special Subject on mid-19th-century France were of a high order. I was lucky to be working under a very sympathetic Head of Department, Charles Mowat. He even went along with my mad cap scheme of a year-long Part I course on moments of revolutionary change: I gave ten lectures on the Russian revolution. (The course was cancelled by Gwilym Usher on his return from America in favour of his original course on mediaeval history.) It was at Bangor that I and a colleague, Emlyn Sherrington, responded to a request from students to widen the syllabus into the Third World and we laid on a course on Aspects of the Third World. I took on Japan, Nigeria and India. When I finally took up an appointment in January 1967 at the University of Kent I was encouraged to pursue these interests. During my first decade at Kent I was drawn into a most exciting teaching experience of inter-disciplinary studies. I saw Kent as a kind of finishing school. My interests gravitated around two big contemporary themes, of decolonisation and sexual liberation. And one of the great virtues of Kent was its readiness to let one teach abroad and its exchange programmes with West Africa and the Caribbean. So after all I taught abroad, at the JNU, New Delhi, for the Monsoon semester 1973 (I was a late replacement for Richard Cobb), and the University of Ibadan 1974-5. I spent a whole year teaching Russian history.

And there I leave it.

11
EPILOGUE

Does the resolution of identity rule out the relevance of the alternatives? Were these in the end but *culs-de-sac*?

I think the possibility of a legal career, my Father's choice, was of this nature. Although I was quite excited by the dramatic possibilities of the Bar when Father's great friend, Edward Iwi, took me at the age of eighteen on a visit to the Old Bailey, I could never have become a lawyer. I always struggled at having to read legal judgments in the course of academic study of constitutional history. I doubt if anything quite so high-minded as Gandhi's mounting distaste at the intellectual dishonesty of legal practice, the need to present false cases for his clients, would have been the reason. I just did not fancy the hair-splitting niceties of the law.

Readers might have become rather tired of my adolescent engagement with the arts. I am no Julian Barnes, so tracing my exploration of European art may be of little interest. However, it is a journey many of us undertake, so it is of some intrinsic interest. I am intrigued to discover the way the clash of a this-worldly aesthetic and other-worldly, shaped by the contrasting outlook of Stephen Spender and T S Eliot at the time, was to be resurrected in later life: it is the theme of my most recent book, a study of 20th century continental music, *Music and the Spiritual: Composers and Politics in the 20th Century*. If I favoured Spender's approach, I was beginning with my awareness of Modernism to go in a new direction and assert the exclusive claims of the work of art. In later life I seem to have been less engaged with the function of the arts.

So did I have the makings of a poet? I lacked the discipline of true craftsmanship. I always fell back on free verse. Many of us are poets in adolescence and maybe my experience was commonplace. Still, I think the poetry is worth the light of day.

Clearly there was an unresolved religious debate in adolescence. I have mentioned my attraction to monasticism and it remains one of the regrets of my life that I was ill-equipped to pursue a monastic vocation. In the same way as Christopher Isherwood, though he at least put it to the test as a Ramakrishna monk, the demands of my sexuality was an impossible barrier. But some of the best experiences of my life were visiting and staying in monastic communities. Whilst at Oxford I was told that if you were religious as a child and adolescent, then there was a high chance you would return to the faith in one's forties; and this was to happen. Maybe only in retirement have religious questions taken centre-stage. At my 70th birthday party I made a speech in which I said the true value of our third age was the chance to finally to come off the fence on whether or not we believe in God and the after-life. And I have been reading literature on near-death experience and the ways in which we might shape our reincarnation.

Should I have become a psychotherapist? I recall moments of intense excitement after seeing films such as *The Deep Blue Sea* and *Suddenly Last Summer*, plays of Terence Rattigan and Tennessee Williams to the fore, when I was hugely animated at the thought of being a therapist to sort out such psychological distress. But maybe all along this was too self-centred, too emotional, and I would have lacked the self-effacement and control to be a therapist. I also think the discipline feeds rather too much off itself, and I might have become rather bored by its narrowness. Still, in my sixties, I approached the Jungian clinic in Zurich to look into the possibility of training as a Jungian, and they were very keen to recruit me.

My greatest dread in life was my having to be a school teacher. So it was a huge relief to realise I had the qualifications to be an academic. All along my strongest subject was History, though English literature in some ways ran it close, and if I never saw it as a vocation, I realised it would always provide an outlet for my curiosity. Admittedly, in Lawrence Stone's wonderful terminology, I was always to be the lepidopterist rather than the truffle hunter, relishing the opportunity to expand horizons, but I was to make serious research forays into both French and Indian history. And as an academic I have naturally been fascinated by the course of my own educational history, so I apologise to those who found my interest in school reports and other academic comment on my degree work rather tedious.

And was my life radically affected by the Oxford trauma? Looking back on my time at the Warneford I realise this was certainly a time when I moved away from religion, and if not immediately, my sense of myself as a poet. I also acquired a greater sense of what was feasible in my life, a greater sense of reality, and in the long run this led to my acceptance of an academic profession. In that sense its influence was paramount. Of course the Warneford experience very nearly turned me into a psychotherapist.

But above all the trauma determined my sexuality. One reader feels Miss Davidson with her attempt to 'turn' me may be at risk of being seen as the villain of the piece. She of course was merely at one with the moral and socio-legal climate of the day and she was in no way about to join the anti-psychiatry movement of Ronnie Laing. In a way the criminal conviction imposed a gay identity on me. Much of my future academic writing was on the history of homosexuality, in books such as *Sexual Moralities in Modern France 1780-1980* and *A Spiritual Bloomsbury.* It was a trauma from which I never wholly recovered and it was to be an absolute taboo subject of conversation. Revisiting the whole experience in this memoir has been painful. But I have seen the need to be a witness to the persecution of the postwar years and I see the memoir as a case-study in homosexuality.

Yet there is a sad paradox. Though I had been literally forced out of the closet I was never socially at ease as a homosexual, I tended to keep my private life to myself, and in a very real sense felt myself marginalised all my life. I was always very reluctant to take on any public role.

I have never been closely involved in practical politics. But it is striking to be reminded in writing of this postwar adolescence the degree to which I was drawn into the Cold War. There was this continuing debate between Christianity and Communism. The threat of National Service and then Officer training enforced a closer reading of contemporary politics than possibly was ever to be the case later on. We were being conditioned into being Cold War warriors. My response was in part shaped by the left-wing sympathies of the romantic poets, Shelley above all, and those of the Thirties, Spender a role model. It also led after my experience of the Cyprus Emergency and Suez to a profound engagement with the history of decolonisation and to a life-time fascination with Gandhi. Maybe I was always more political than I realised.

In Italian history the period of the Risorgimento is seen as a period of poetry in contrast to post-Risorgimento as a period of prose. I guess this is true of adolescence and post-adolescence. Probably all hormonal. Adulthood necessarily feels flatter. Mine was an adolescence with more than its fair share of conflict and anguish, but one of sustained interest and one hugely varied. But writing this memoir suggests that life comes full circle and many of the problems of adolescence come back to haunt us.

Coda

But there is more to say. Memoirs betray more than they intend. Two members of the psychotherapeutic community have looked at the memoir and come up with very different readings. Here is the first.

Some discouraging home-truths can be read into the memoir. This is a very perceptive but highly critical reading. It is seen in terms of a tension between a search for recognition as an academic and a conflicting need to be true to one's self, or 'coming out'. Not just in terms of my sexuality but some deeper truthfulness to my feelings, 'a coming home'. In a way this tension is perfectly reflected in terms of the two central themes of the memoir, my becoming an academic historian and my coming to terms with my sexuality. The memoir is characterised by detachment. Have I been as honest as I should have been?

So the uncomfortable truth is suggested that my choice of career as an academic was a kind of flight from a truthfulness to myself. Maybe all along I was programmed to seek some sort of public recognition at whatever cost to my true feelings. My intense competitiveness at both preparatory and public school, my applying to be an Officer in National Service - is all clear evidence of this. This memoir concedes that I was aware that the trajectory of my life at Oxford, my reaction to my trauma, was leading me away from that highly personal sense of myself as a poet and my engagement with religion.

In fact, and here to rebut this interpretation, I was never to be very clever at the pursuit of public recognition. I was a poor academic politician, fought shy of administration, and only at the ripe old age of 78 did the University of Kent confer on me the title of Honorary Professor of Modern European and Indian History. I tended to give way to more ambitious colleagues. But at a wider level this is all about the choice we make between the public and the private sphere.

But does all this indicate that there was a failure to engage with the emotions? A fatal detachment? Here I have to revisit the therapy at Warneford. Had I been encouraged to accept myself as gay then at the very least I would have been honest about 'coming out' and I would have sustained a far more truthful relationship with friends and company generally. Was all this part, though, of a greater failure to be truthful to my self? It raises the sad possibility that for most of my life I only half-lived, was never wholly open, and, indeed, I certainly kept my private life separate from my public university life.

But the second response is far kinder. How could I have been expected to be 'truthful' to an identity I was indeed still searching for? The memoir is all about that quest. Keeping journals was a way of constantly checking against self-deception and being as truthful as I could at the time. 'Coming out' at a time when homosexuality was still criminal would anyway have been high risk. Maybe Dr Scottowe and May Davidson were simply trying to steer me away from criminal activity. A David Hockney might have got away with being an out gay but not necessarily a provincial University lecturer in North Wales.

I myself cannot see any harm in detachment. I simply wonder if any of us ever achieve true transparency and whether I could in all honesty have lived my life any other way.

Were I to write a subsequent volume on adulthood I could further pursue, as the first commentator would see it, this redemptive process. I have a huge correspondence with family, friends and lovers and it is clear that in a very Forsterian and Bloomsbury way I privileged this private sphere over the public. But, at the same time, I'm aware how often I held back in family relationships and was less than honest with some friends. This could cause unhappiness and much confusion. One is always confronted by the limits of truthfulness.

Appendix
POETRY

A Dream

I dreamt of a far distant land, a dream
In the night, when verduous wilds of green
Became my dwelling place. A lordly
Domain, high, high amidst mountains, chilly
But glistening in a sun that shone
Through the evergreen trees of my home
Mine was a wild resort, deserted and alone
Without so much as a moan
Of a wind bewildered from Aeolian lands
No noise was there of shepherd bands
Whose music once did mingle with the air
For I was alone in my mountainous lair

(Published anon in *The Grasshopper* 1954.
My only published poem.)

Listening to Cesar Frank's Symphony

Where are the boundaries to Eternity?
There are no rocks to wound a soul's sensibility
Like those rocks held scythe-like by the sea
Which tear the hearts of innocent ships
But is there no harbour to rest
From her wanderings, interminable as death?
Often when the mind escapes the need for thought
In its frailty born away by music's stream
To worlds unseen by unsympathetic souls
It penetrates deep night

Perceives that light of childish dreams
Yet the soul senses void and emptiness
Music, relation of divinity
Reveals that God to impatient souls
May it flood the emptiness of heaven
Like music fills the tired soul
Or an evening breeze a forest lulled by day
But do not leave the soul mid- air
Like a leaf tossed by indifferent winds

On Visiting a Church in Stoke Newington

You lived in a dingy house
But when you opened the door
I saw happiness in your eyes
And I was content with your contentment
Then we walked through this world
Unknown to one pampered by social position
Down to the church hall where children played
Under the shadow of the dark church
I looked deep into those children's eyes
Saw they were not wholly innocent
They knew of petty sins readily accepted
But I knew from that too ready acceptance
Shining from bright eyes under the shadow of the church
They were ignorant of vaster shadows
Enveloping the world with immense damnation
But I felt someone shared my knowledge
No it was not you with your bright confidence
But the dark church begrimed with our sins
A perpetual and horrible reminder of our sins

Moth in a Red Vase

I see a moth asleep in a red vase
As red as any eastern sun
Scattered with flowers in a Chinese pattern
White flowers afloat on a purple wine

Lotus leaves asleep on a pool
Burning red in an eastern sun
And the moth, a dark silhouette
Wings as sleek and smooth as sleep
Clear against a red glass sky
A moth in her search for rest
From lustful lights
Fell asleep in a red fire
Fed by passing clouds and the sky
A red fire burning eternally
How can you be so peaceful, drowsing moth
When you dwell in a land of such eternal fire
A land of flames that recall the dying sun
Land of rich wine, gaiety and song
And then I knew that the dark moth was dead
All night she must have struggled here
Scorning those delights, longing for the cold night air
Until the dawn took pity on its tiny heart
And gave her a final rest

Martyrdom

Will the impetuous youth run away to Africa
And love the black race with the hatred of his own
Playing Christ the charlatan and crying kill kill kill
In tortured tread towards his self-created Golgotha
And how do you regard this Nazerene more suffering and pale
Than the gentle God who turned the Dead Sea into salt
Do you the rich, successful, laugh away his dreadful dreams
In idle drives across savannah on the asphalt way?

Cyprus 1956

Rest you heathen gods
Whose vision far outstrips the farthest sea
Curling away to eternity

Why must you trouble so these lands?
Why arrogant sires raise your heads
Swathed in snakes that lash like whips of Xerxes
The sea of man's desires?
In an island grown vast with terror
I stress the need for us to stand remote
Never let the mountain mists blur our vision
View the hills with impartial eyes
You with your stories of atrocities stir hatred in my heart
The hatred of a child who destroys
A toy he dearly prized
These we must accept
Some hundred desperate men
An anxious innocent population
But I ask us to revoke that spirit of revenge
That sweeps through hearts as swift as fire
Greedily licks its tongue into the green valley
Envelops lives in its cruel flames
But you the proud ones ignore my pleading
I see you turn and stare at the tireless sea
I hear you scream against the indifferent wind
O foolish young man
We are the brave and young
We usurp the parchment papered land
Scroll with tongues of fire against the sky
Our epic of the future
Step with us across the dance-floor of the world
Clad in vivid clothes
Smile with white and brilliant teeth
And listen to our tale

Boarding Party

Mysterious and elusive
Two dark birds scour the evening sky
Where the sun flaunts her scarlet death
Eagerly they stare at the boat

Stabbed by searchlight
Sailors, visiting soldiers, all one
In their vulgar curiosity
Meanwhile in the calm straightforward British way
The boarding party clamber into the boat
And set out towards the pinioned fishing craft
Across the indifferent sea
I stand alone in my indecision
Staring at the low flung coastline
Which they so utterly disregard
I stare and I think of Cape Greco, the rock that renounced
the sea
To rise massive and proud
Into the frail blue Mediterranean sky

The Turk and the Divided Self

Come away, come away, dangerous indecisive heart
You mark your man too closely
As he walks through the twisted ancient tress
Do you admire his easy gait?
Come away, come away for sin is all too tempting
And you are surely weak
And where shall I go to pray?
Can I not admire a handsome workman with a well -
tanned face?
You are too suspicious sir, go, leave me in peace
Come away, come away with me into the falling light
Walk with me into the approaching night
Behold the day's sacrifice of the sun
On the altar of the dark and clear-cut mountains
Surely now you forget your desires
Quiet, he comes. No longer now do branches
That imagination could not tear aside
Mar his visage. Ah, sir, here is beauty, sensuous, desirable
Grant me the pleasure of my eyes
Now divided heart, which way do you turn?

I will leave you as your desire stands
So beautiful and strong against the horizon
And the outspent dusk

Listening to Shura Cherkassky

However we shape our lives
Sculpt the pattern out of ivory
Feel the form with crayon
Beware of the mould
For that is not our making
See the mould as a clumsy carpenter
Rough blows of the chisel
Misplaced sandpaper
Never be his subject

Assisi

This was the cloud burst. Streets yellow
With lightning, the white stroke in the sky
A prayer for sunlight. People pursed their lips
Jerked their oilskins high over their summer-burnt necks
The cloud laughed, spat rivers on the land
The jungle village yelped dark animals
The tiger slunk from the church façade
And scowled in the gloom

Worcester College Gardens

The entirety of day-all I wish to describe
But one passage of time alone in the garden
Aware of clusters of twigs, nest of bird
Amongst the language of tree scribbled in the sky
Knowing no permanence in song of bird
Merely an unusual strength, a carefree rebellion
No withdrawn hate revealed in scarred battle
But relaxation with no remorse and no fear
A communion. Not one bird but all, shaking

The branch, lake, gardener, my own heart
Feeling the hidden grief and mocking its secrecy
Charging heart to sing like the white tongued oak
To relate this joy to the pastel grey of dusk
The pink haze cut by the songless branch
And I seeing figure of man drunk with day
Turn blank-eyed to bright street and town
Where no one knows the song of bird or tongue of fire
No one even sees that ghostly tower and spire of town
Nor retain the song of day. They welcome night
The sun falls out of the empty skull

Betrayal

I admit the commonplaceness of our meeting
The shallow beginning of our friendship
And yet surely we knew this was only a beginning
And time was necessary to sunder deep our loyalty
Now you have already departed
Presumably content with this empty affair
Satisfied by the tepid love of a moment
And am I fair to scathe you now for your dishonesty?
You promised we should meet again
I accepted and left - oh may I be ready then for the end
But the passing night reminded me of your embrace
And I know no single meeting could efface
The longing for a deeper understanding
Several simple things about you that I love
The growl of your voice, the boot leather of your face
Those furrowed facial lines and brilliant blue of eyes
Surely you would write again and let me know
I was worth more than the snatched pleasure of a night
How else can I interpret your silence than disgrace?
Am I one to laugh at loneliness
And sit high towered mocking isolation
Do I welcome the possibility of grief?
Do I relish the chance of pain?

No, no I merely wish to see you smiling once again
And know that smile is meant for me
I only wish to feel your hand locked in mine
And know our love is blessed with permanence
Maybe just another meeting, a chance to explain
To talk of understanding, of levels of existence
And sense we can move beyond our visual pain
Into the unusual haven of an anchored love

An Enquiry

If you were to ask me now
Yes as a frank enquiry
What do you believe in?
I should be most confused
Stumbling through thorned branches and unharvested
field
I should remember my ecstatic race through the yellow
heaven
Chasing the wild and graceful bird
With his unpinioned wing
If I were then asked
What do you mean by freedom?
I should have said, the untrammelled journey
Of the heart

Greece

Cupped and lanced by a sun of falling light
The broken landscape dies
Beyond the reach of human tears
In the furrowed silences of night
Clusters of light of the city
Infirm statements of the human will
Occasional, purposeful, a well-lit street
Only an intrepid visionary asks where
If you remember the Greek race
Live under the shadow of Sultan and Basileus

You will divine her ethos correct
As that of a subject race.
A white nun rose from the brown earth
And fled across the gaunt skull of land
Till she came to the deeply burrowed well of love
Where she plied her hand in vain.
Crying yet tearless she upbraids the wind
Calcine, allows the sparse sand
To sting her white flesh, regards the sun
More dark than any aborigine.
Now she ran with steps as fleet as any thirsty hart
Till she came to the dark sprawling plain
Of lonely rocks wherein the hermit kept his cell.

And one came back, a survivor from America
And told us the empty-headed, with massive clarity,
Of Eden and Jerusalem and I knew then
All dreams of Elysium were vain.

Her prayer, the language of a child
Inconsequential, fresh, an unusual figure
Kneeling on the sand, comparing perpetuity of sea
To the change of human life
Like a besetting tune more hypnotic
Than any strange call of ancient drum
Or flute in sacred grove
Calls desire, flee the acknowledged truth
Bury the flaming torch in the entangling byre

Bird-lore

Let the mind fall into the psychic undertow
Of birds flocking westward to the heathen mountains
There echoes of the dark cry of the ghosted land.
In the figures of bird flight a folk-lore is written
More absolute than any ancient myth or religion
Wiser than any reasoning or system.
You need a special vision to understand

Its endless shifting hieroglyphs
A truth whose darkness defied the hermit
The social worker, even the expert in dreams
Grew hesitant at any explanation
No type of person is qualified as interpreter
It requires a special flexibility of mind
To tear back the cramping wisdom of the west
To flow into the instinct of the bird
In its curving flight and sudden darkness
And disappearance in the molten sun
The terrible whiteness a reminder of the purity
Of the first world and the great challenge
That Adam gave to God. But the birds ignore
The human quest and grew beyond construction
Into a perfect knowledge of truth
To flow into the flight of a bird

Mykonos

Then you and I danced the rooftops of whitewashed
    houses
The sun the colour of cobweb cloaking the rocks
The sense of freedom in the serge dusk
I leapt the wall and sang mock poetry of Mayakovsky
Till the great world turned into night
You and I were always strangers
Only in this hour did we play
The game of lovers, I the narcissist
Pleased by your desire
A sprite alive in this turning hour
Too light for the bright day
Too transparent for the solid dark
Now dancing the rooftops rejoicing
You the pathetic beggar, riding into nowhere
But later you showed the strength of the true dancer
One who joined the transcendent flesh
In the giant tournament of the hunter

That wild prey of the night

A New Language

You want a new language
Containing the doldrum speech of man
And the cruel words of machinery
Nothing of latterday romance
But poetry all the same
To lift our language from the rut of ill-considered speech
That ugly practicality of conversation
You cannot pretend that we speak poetry
We who only talk of our unpoetic lives
But to suggest the sudden leap
From pattern of prose to the quicksand metre of poetry
Then we tremble and fall into a new relationship
Minds achieve a new daring

Brief Encounter

Moving through a dark shadowland
I feel for an alien lover
All the strangled love of the lunatic
For logic

Untitled

Long languish in the tension
Where they meet above your eyes
Curl about the furled lip
Above the brush of your smile
I was never there but trailed
The very split of your hair
Po Paidikon as I was
Never trust to any idée fixe
But clever as that same curl of wit
Senex mon semblable mon frére
No undistinguishable plan can

Descry ever under plain wrappers
The news I bring skipping
With my mother's umbilicus
Praise God for applied things
Precocious pippin piping hot
You give so much
I could never hope or want it all
But there is some tea for me

She got up afraid of their misunderstanding
Would they smile at her pock-marked skin
High in the apple tree playing with the boys
Of childhood. They were no inquisitors of her shy mind
Now she went in dread of their callous stare
In the spring her father had said 'your bicycle
Go now, play'. Emblazoned by pride she sped
Down the chute of the hill into a vast circus
Of astonishing delight recognising in her liberty
The flight of the trapeze artist, the camaraderie
Of the acrobat. Then no hesitancy, no fear
Of the full blooded call of youth
Fortunate pierrot, your permanent disguise
Of pallid skin. You move sad puppet
Strung to all the melancholy of your audience
Yet beautiful in your disguise
She moves beneath the frosted branch and frozen sky

(I suspect I did not write the first part of this poem.)

Some Readers' Responses

Professor Rod Kedward writes:

A fascinating memoir, especially for contemporaries, which offers intimate insight into the search for vocational and sexual identity across vulnerable years of private education and Oxford scholarships, much of it captured in an intensely personal diary. The cruel and moving trauma of arrest and exposure at the heart of the story makes for a wider social significance, as does the colourful experience and critique of National Service at the time of Suez. The cultural quest and poetic expression of a highly self-conscious young intellectual will be both demanding and revealing for sympathetic readers.

The Revd Hugh Maddox writes:

An intriguing story in which Professor Copley tells of his difficult childhood with touching openness and honesty; an intelligent and highly sensitive child, he suffered both at school and at home as his parents moved towards divorce. He sees his motives and emotions with analytical accuracy but this does not feel self-indulgent. From his last year at school and on to Oxford his knowledge and appreciation of art, music and literature is phenomenal and it is fascinating to see the effect they have on each other, and, most unusually, on his own personal life and thought.

He tells of the different world of National Service commission in the Royal Navy at the time of the Suez invasion, followed by the social world of Malta.

The climax of the book is his arrest following police entrapment for gross indecency. This led to a shattering breakdown and time in the Warneford hospital. It is important to read of the devastating reaction of a highly sensitive and intelligent scholar to cruel laws, still existing in the sixties. A book well worth reading.

Dr Neil Cheshire writes:

Professor Copley's courageously intimate survey of the first two decades or so of his life reflects on a series of emotional crises, some of which are harrowing and all of which challenged some aspect of his emerging sense of identity. We are led from early self-questioning about his intellectual and athletic talents, through life-long debates about psychosexual identity, spirituality and potential role-models amongst modern writers he admired, up to the reluctant part he played perforce in the Suez crisis of 1956. On the way we encounter unnerving vicissitudes of 'the Freudian family romance', maternal deprivation at going to boarding school at the age of seven, his negative Oedipus complex and his parent's divorce.

One of these crises saw him admitted as an undergraduate to a local psychiatric hospital where he experienced two contrasting types of treatment. One was an old-fashioned chemical procedure already being questioned in the medical literature of the day and soon to be discredited, the other a pioneering amalgam of eclectic psychotherapy and academic counselling dispensed by a remarkable woman who was a founder member of the fledgling profession of Clinical Psychologist.

That this troubled boy and young man somehow survived to become an accomplished academic historian is a tribute to his friends and helpers as well as to his own resilience and resourcefulness. As such, Copley's story will offer help and comfort to any who find themselves similarly troubled today.

* 9 7 8 1 7 8 4 5 6 2 9 7 7 *

ND - #0174 - 060826 - C0 - 216/138/20 - PB - 9781784562977 - Gloss Lamination